VIENNESE
DESIGN
AND THE
WIENER
WERKSTÄTTE

Viennese Design and the Wiener Werkstätte

By Jane Kallir

With a Foreword by Carl E. Schorske

Galerie St. Etienne/George Braziller, New York

Exhibition dates:
September 23–November 8, 1986
Galerie St. Etienne
24 West 57th Street
New York, New York 10019

Published in 1986 by Galerie St. Etienne/George Braziller

Library of Congress Cataloguing-in-Publication Data

Kallir, Jane.
    Viennese design and the Wiener Werkstätte.

    1. Wiener Werkstätte. 2. Decorative arts—
Austria—Vienna—History—20th century. I. Galerie
St. Etienne. II. Title.
NK945.V53K34 1986   745′.09436′13   86—915
ISBN 0–8076–1154–9
ISBN 0–8076–1153–0 (pbk.)

Designed by Gary Cosimini
Printed and bound in Japan

Cover: Maria Likarz. Fashion design. Color lithograph postcard (No. 769). 5½″ × 3½″. Published by the Wiener Werkstätte.

CREDITS:
Joh. Backhausen & Söhne (fig. 135); Beethoven exhibition catalogue, Secession (figs. 61. 164); Christie, Manson and Woods, International, Inc. (pl. 5; figs. 10, 11); *Deutsche Kunst und Dekoration* (figs. 3, 8, 20, 27, 36, 47, 49, 50, 52, 54, 55, 56, 57, 60, 66, 67, 69, 72, 73, 118, 126, 127, 128, 132, 133, 188); Max Eisler, *Dagobert Peche* (figs. 28, 119, 146, 149); Fischer Fine Art, Ltd. (figs. 44, 100, 106, 111, 136, 160, 168, 170); Barry Friedman, Ltd. (pls. 1, 8, 13, 15, 16, 18, 19, 52; figs. 12, 14, 53, 76, 86, 88, 89, 91, 94, 97, 104, 149, 185, 186); Gwathmey Siegel & Associates, Architects (figs. 5, 6); Tiroler Landesmuseum Ferdinandeum, Innsbruck (fig. 184); *Das Interieur* (fig. 38); Knoll International, Inc. (fig. 7); Rudolf von Larisch, *Beispiele künstlerischer Schrift* (fig. 163); J. & L. Lobmeyr (fig. 103); The James May Collection (pls. 34, 35, 36; figs. 122, 124, 138, 139, 140, 141, 142, 143, 144, 145); Galerie Metropol, Inc. (pl. 21; figs. 22, 74, 174); Gallery Modernism (pl. 21; figs. 35, 81, 84); Lillian Nassau, Ltd. (pls. 22, 25, 27, 28; figs. 109, 153, 158); the Metropolitan Museum of Art, New York (fig. 31); the Museum of Modern Art, New York (pls. 20, 48; figs. 19, 101, 105); Eduard F. Sekler (Frontispiece; figs. 37, 51, 58, 59); the Shepherd Gallery (pl. 50; figs. 16, 96, 159, 173, 180); *The Studio* (figs. 87, 137); Unika Vaev/I. C. F., Inc. (fig. 134); *Ver Sacrum* (figs. 2, 15, 17, 46, 62, 63, 161, 162, 171, 172, 175); the Historisches Museum der Stadt Wien, Vienna (pls. 11, 29; figs. 1, 4, 41, 42, 43, 48, 64, 107, 108, 123, 125, 154, 169); the Österreichische Galerie, Vienna (pls. 47, 53, 54); the Österreichisches Museum für angewandte Kunst, Vienna (pls. 2, 3, 4, 12, 17, 30, 41, 42; figs. 75, 82, 83, 90, 93, 98, 102, 112, 113, 115, 117, 129, 130, 131, 176, 177, 187); the Österreichische Nationalbibliothek, Vienna (figs. 13, 21, 23, 24, 61); the Phillips Collection, Washington, D. C. (pl. 55); Wiener Werkstätte sales catalogue, 1923 (fig. 147); *25 Jahre Wiener Werkstätte* (figs. 151, 152); Christopher Wilk (figs. 77, 79); Woka/ Wolfgang Karolinsky (fig. 99).

Photography by Geoffrey Clements (pls. 22, 25, 26, 27); Galerie St. Etienne (figs. 3, 8, 9, 20, 27, 36, 45, 47, 49, 50, 52, 54, 55, 56, 57, 61, 66, 67, 69, 72, 73, 85, 118, 122, 124, 126, 127, 128, 130, 131, 138, 139, 140, 141, 142, 143, 144, 145, 157, 165, 188); Margery King (figs. 2, 15, 16, 17, 26, 28, 46, 60, 62, 63, 68, 70, 76, 87, 109, 114, 119, 120, 134, 137, 146, 148, 151, 152, 153, 156, 159, 161, 162, 163, 164, 171, 172, 173, 175, 178, 179, 180, 181, 182, 183, 189); Joseph McDonald (pls. 23, 24, 28, 33, 37, 38, 40; figs. 33, 92, 116, 121); Norman McGrath (figs. 5, 6); Eric Pollitzer (cover; pls. 7, 9, 10, 31, 32, 34, 35, 36, 43, 44, 45, 46, 49, 50); Ritter (frontispiece; figs. 58, 59); Susie Wileman (pls. 6, 39; figs. 40, 95).

Frontispiece: Josef Hoffmann. Palais Stoclet, Brussels; front façade. 1905–11.

CONTENTS

1. Gustav Klimt. Poster for
the first Secession exhibition.
1898. Color lithograph.
38¼″ × 27½″.

FOREWORD

In the last quarter of the nineteenth century—first in politics, then in literature and finally, with the "Secession," in the visual arts—*die Jungen*, a young generation of Viennese intellectuals, rose in a succession of revolts against the alleged falsity of their fathers' liberal culture. Everywhere they proclaimed their break from the past, the autonomy of modernity against history. Thus on the pediment of the Secession's building, the rebels engraved as motto, "To the age its art; to art its freedom." And as the title for their newly founded journal, the young artists chose the Latin phrase *Ver Sacrum* — sacred spring—to proclaim their aim of cultural renewal (fig. 2).

The aggressive vigor of the young rebels was made explicit by the painter Gustav Klimt in his poster for the Secession's first exhibition in 1898 (fig. 1). No mere art show was announced here, but a dramatic action of wider import for society. Klimt, good Austrian that he was, had pictorial recourse to his culture's favorite art form, the theater, to convey his message. His poster shows Athena, protectrix of the people (her statue was about to be placed before the Austrian parliament building), presiding over a scene of deadly struggle. Theseus, champion of youth, plunges his sword into the Minotaur, the man-beast who has kept the children of Athens in bondage. And on the curtains flanking his poster's "stage," Klimt inscribed the new movement's slogan: "*Ver Sacrum*." Thus was the struggle of Austria's rebellious sons to throw off the shackles of their elders and of history allegorized.

In the bliss of the Secession's dawn, the men and women who would soon make the Wiener Werkstätte—artists, patrons and consumers—found their mission and acquired their form. They were electrified by the prospect of creating through art a new public culture, a *theatrum mundi* (theater of the world) at once modern and beautiful. In the beginning, this aim was connected with another, more philosophical and introspective: to explore through art and intellect the nature of modern man. For this quest, too, Gustav Klimt provided an icon in his drawing of *Nuda Veritas*: literally, naked truth personified as a nubile waif holding up a mirror to modern man. At first the two aims—to create a new, modern beauty, and to disclose a new existential truth—were pur-

2. Alfred Roller. Cover of the first issue of *Ver Sacrum*. 1898.

3

sued as part of the same enterprise. But soon there appeared in the mirror of *Nuda Veritas* an image of modern man not easily harmonized with the beautiful environment to which the Art Nouveau of the period aspired: a man driven by instinct, by Eros and Thanatos (sex and death). First revealed in Nietzschean affirmation, this psychological man was soon perceived and assessed in ambivalence and pain. The best artists—Klimt in painting, Schnitzler and Hofmannsthal in literature, Zemlinsky and Mahler in music, and Freud in science—found themselves participating less in the Sacred Spring of communal regeneration than in a somber autumn of personal introspection in a social world running out of orbit and beyond control.

In the contradiction-laden atmosphere that characterized Vienna's burst into the modern era, what was the place and nature of the applied arts? A partial answer may be found in the concept of the *Gesamtkunstwerk* (total artwork), which derived from *die Jungen*'s admiration of Richard Wagner's theatrical ideal as a model for a communitarian future. In Austria, the *Gesamtkunstwerk* drew even deeper sustenance from a still vital baroque tradition, which accorded primacy to theatrical representations in all the arts: to opera over symphony in music, to theater over the novel in literature, and to architecture over painting in the plastic arts. The men who launched the Wiener Werkstätte in 1903 merely extended this tradition in the visual realm. Thus Klimt was trained and won his spurs as a decorator of architecture, and the architect Josef Hoffmann thought of buildings as works of visual art

in which interior and exterior were unified by a common expressivity. These artists developed a new integrated aesthetic wherein painting became just one component of a total design scheme, and architecture was enriched and made whole by the coordination of all subordinate detailing.

Just at the time when the Secession launched its mission to revitalize culture, the possibility of great public projects evaporated. The Ringstrasse—the long circular boulevard surrounding Vienna's inner city—had been developed in the mid-nineteenth century as an urban *Gesamtkunstwerk* in the baroque spirit. It had so thoroughly fulfilled the elite's need and desire for monumental civic building in the capital that when a new generation of architects came along at the century's close, they were cast back upon private residences as virtually their only professional outlet. Painters, architects and designers found that they could best realize their shared aspirations to the total artwork by creating luxury dwellings for clients of wealth and aesthetic sensibility.

This economically enforced turn from the public to the private sphere as the scene of the *Gesamtkunstwerk* found reinforcement in the new introspective culture heralded by the image of psychological man reflected in the mirror of Klimt's *Nuda Veritas*. Not that the designers followed Nietzsche and Freud to the murky depths whence sprang the wells of instinct, as the Expressionist painters did (fig. 4). But they, too, served the new man of feeling (*Gefühlsmensch*) through a process of sublimation, whereby the power of instinct became transmuted into the refined aesthetic sensibility of

3. Josef Hoffmann and Koloman Moser. Dining room
designed for Editha Mautner-
Markhof, Vienna. 1904.

4. Oskar Kokoschka. *Pietà*
(poster for the Kunstschau
theater). 1909. Color lithograph. 49½″ × 31⅞″.

the educated self. In their greatest collaborative works, the artists of the Wiener Werkstätte created an integrated environment, a house beautiful with all its attendant-use objects, for those who aspired to a new kind of personalized life beautiful (figs. 3 and 58). Where the man of high culture of the mid-nineteenth century enriched his life with the works of the past, his "modern" successor was expected to define himself from within, to refine his own psyche into art. The forms and objects of living—the house, its furnishings, its art— were to be personal expressions of each man's soul and beauty. The architects and designers freed their own poetic fantasies to create the images and design motifs that would satisfy this need. "In [my] house," wrote Hermann Bahr, one of the literary champions for the new art, "I should everywhere be able to see my soul as in a mirror." The theater of the world here shrank to the theater of the narcissistic self. Thus the Secession's Sacred Spring of general cultural renewal issued in the luxuriant summer of the Wiener Werkstätte, with its *Gesamtkunstwerk* for tasteful living and its personalized production of objects for a clientele of connoisseurs.

Jane Kallir's comprehensive work traces the fascinating trajectory of the Wiener Werkstätte over three decades, from its initial attempt to create a holistic and harmonious living environment, to its fragmentation by the need to produce a multitude of modish artifacts. Kallir stresses as has none before her the rootedness of this arts-and-crafts movement in the ideal of the *Gesamtkunstwerk*. Additionally, she not only charts the rise, flowering and decay of the Wiener Werkstätte, but assesses its extraordinary artistic achievements in every branch of design. In so doing, the author analyzes for the first time the dense web of connections —institutional and educational, intellectual and social—that enabled the imaginative leaders of the Werkstätte to impress upon the Austrian elite and the world beyond their visual ideals and stylistic idiom. Even though these men had to abandon their original hopes of a comprehensive transformation of culture through art, their ideals lived on and may be seen as the basis for much of the subsequent modernist tradition. —*Carl E. Schorske*

5. Gwathmey Siegel & Associates, Architects. Private residence, East Hampton, New York; screened porch. 1979. Seating group designed by Hans Vollmer (1902).

INTRODUCTION

The mystique of *fin-de-siècle* Vienna has, in recent years, acquired a rather powerful hold on the American imagination, engendering a spate of publications and exhibitions whose ramifications have reached all the way to Vienna and ricocheted back through Europe. It is perhaps natural that, as we approach our own *fin de siècle*, the turn of the previous century should evoke renewed interest. Beyond this, as the modern movement—which has been possessed of a longevity that almost belies the meaning of the term—seems finally to be reaching its end, the inevitable process of revisionism and reevaluation has begun.

Foremost among the biases requiring adjustment is the effective cultural blockade that two world wars imposed upon the Germanic tradition. Austria, whose cultural and political identity was so often subsumed by that of her more aggressive neighbor, has been even longer in reclaiming her rightful place in the history of modern art. Additionally, the body of critical literature that grew up around postwar American painting posited a theoretical dependence on French formal values, equating progress with abstraction and leaving little room for the figural expressionism that flourished in Germany and Austria.

Just as we are rediscovering the figure in the painting of both the present and the past, so too, in design, the era of "postmodernism" has ushered in a more flexible interpretation of the earlier modernist canon. While the so-called postmodern architects have resurrected a heritage of historical forms that had been taboo in enlightened circles for nearly a century, other architects have investigated the origins of modernism itself in order to reintroduce a note of intimacy to a tradition that had grown increasingly austere and impersonal. Within this context, the work of Josef Hoffmann and Koloman Moser, who in 1903 cofounded the Wiener Werkstätte (Vienna Workshop), has attracted considerable attention on the part of architects, designers and collectors. Whereas much twentieth-century furniture design concentrated on melding form and construction within a single unified entity, Hoffmann and Moser, while anticipating concerns such as functionalism and integrity in the use of materials, still applied geometric shapes in a decorative manner. Gwathmey Siegel & Associates is among the present-day architectural firms that have pioneered the Viennese revival. Glass bricks and custom woodwork echo favorite Wiener Werkstätte motifs, such as the square, creating a point of transition between delicate period furniture and the majestic space (fig. 5). Furniture designed by Gwathmey Siegel to coordinate with Viennese pieces focuses on a related use of geometric forms as decorative elements (fig. 6). Many contemporary furniture designers, especially in Italy, have tried to emulate the Viennese look. Richard Meier's series of tables and chairs for Knoll International (fig. 7), like the Wiener Werkstätte designs that inspired it, has a versatility that allows it to be used in varying combinations with conventional modern furnishings and interiors. Both Meier and Gwathmey Siegel have designed ancillary items such as china, glassware and bowls that continue their exploration of Wiener Werkstätte motifs. The idea is not so much to create a completely coordinated system of furnishings and accessories as to widen and thereby enrich the modernist vocabulary.

Would Josef Hoffmann and Koloman Moser be happy about all this? Probably not, or at least not entirely. For Hoffmann, furniture design was an outgrowth of architecture. The chairs and settees in his rooms, no less than the wall coverings, carpets, lighting fixtures, knickknacks and, in extreme cases, even the slippers on the owner's feet, were intended to reflect a total design concept, dictated from the inside out and the outside in. "I believe that a house should appear like a hollow cast and that its exterior must already reveal its interior," he stated. "This applies just as necessarily to the style of each single piece of furniture.... Everything should adhere to the same principle."[1] While today's Wiener Werkstätte "look," at its best, evidences a concern with integral design that is not entirely alien to Hoffmann's, there is no escaping the fact that the period pieces are being presented out of the context for which they were originally intended.

Any dialogue between the present and the past is inevita-

6. Gwathmey Siegel & Associates, Architects. Private residence, East Hampton, New York; bedroom. 1979. Bed designed by Charles Gwathmey; dressing table and chair by Josef Hoffmann (1905).

7. Richard Meier. Furniture collection designed for Knoll International. 1978–82.

6

bly conditioned by the perspective of the present, and the current surge of interest in *fin-de-siècle* Viennese art and design often reveals more about the 1980s than it does about the early 1900s. The period romantically dubbed the "twilight of the Habsburg monarchy" continues to fascinate in our postatomic age because we feel an affinity for a doomed culture, and a hopeful awe that this culture could produce such giants as Freud, Wittgenstein, Mahler, Schoenberg, Klimt, Schiele, Hoffmann, Loos, Hofmannsthal and Rilke. We select, from the biographies of these heroes, those aspects most suited to the creation of a contemporary myth, and conveniently ignore the highly idiosyncratic sociohistorical circumstances that produced them. Similarly, our choices from among the vast array of objects produced by the Wiener Werkstätte during its almost thirty-year history hover around those items conceived in the formative period prior to 1910, because it is these designs that bear the closest relationship to modernism as it developed later in the century. In the process, not only is a considerable amount of interesting material ignored, but the broader achievements of the Wiener Werkstätte remain largely undocumented and misunderstood; like the furniture that is its most visible legacy, it is presented out of context and therefore, out of focus.

The Wiener Werkstätte, which has its roots in the Biedermeier period of the early nineteenth century and extends to the Hitler era of the 1930s, spans a period of time that both precedes and supersedes Vienna's heyday as a center for artistic and intellectual ferment. The Werkstätte thus provides a congenial historical focus for a study of the *fin-de-siècle* phenomenon, for it demands an investigation both of nineteenth-century antecedents and of the general decline that followed World War I. Without proper explanation of the "before" and "after," it can all too easily appear that the Viennese cultural renaissance was an isolated occurrence—a miraculous phenomenon that simply appeared out of thin air

and vanished the same way. Of particular relevance in this endeavor is the period between the wars (what Austrians call the *Zwischenkriegszeit*), for the death of the phenomenon provides important clues as to its genesis: in its end is its beginning, and vice versa.

One of the challenges facing any study that attempts to chronicle the history of Viennese design in the early twentieth century is the vast scope of the subject. A painter, regardless of sporadic social contact with colleagues and patrons, works in solitude; a crafts collective such as the Wiener Werkstätte is by nature communal, both in its internal organization and in its role as a commercial intermediary linking artist/craftsmen with society at large. Thus the Wiener Werkstätte serves as a model of Viennese society in microcosm, reflecting not just the artistic, but also the economic, social and political circumstances of the era. The complexity of this situation is further increased by the broad range of the Werkstätte's activities, for in the organization's self-proclaimed desire to create a *Gesamtkunstwerk* (total artwork), it ventured fearlessly into every field of creative endeavor, from architecture and furniture to textile and fashion design, from wallpaper to wall paintings. Finally, through their connections with Vienna's Kunstgewerbeschule (School of Arts and Crafts), the leaders of the Wiener Werkstätte established a chain of influence that ran through the lives of all the major artistic innovators of prewar Vienna and continued well beyond the organization's official liquidation in 1932. There is hardly an aspect of life or art that the Wiener Werkstätte did not touch, hardly an artist who, growing up in Vienna in the years before World War I, was not in some way affected by it.

Despite the present interest in turn-of-the-century Austria, the field of design, curiously, has not been the subject of a properly analytical or synthetic study. One reason for this may be the relative inaccessibility of the voluminous

7

archives of the Wiener Werkstätte, which are housed at the Österreichisches Museum für angewandte Kunst (Austrian Museum of Applied Art) in Vienna. However, the piecemeal cataloguing and publication of this material has progressed enormously in recent years, so that even if certain dates and facts remain hazy, it is at long last possible to grapple with the multiarmed beast that was the Wiener Werkstätte. The purpose of the present study then, is twofold: first, to present a historical overview of the Wiener Werkstätte and related design trends that is both readily intelligible and that places the movement within the context of other contemporaneous artistic and sociological developments; and second, to establish an easily accessible guide to the seemingly infinite variety of products manufactured by or under the auspices of the Werkstätte and its artists. To this end, the ideological and factual history of the Wiener Werkstätte has been treated in the first two chapters, separately from the aesthetic history that is covered in the remainder of the book. The chapters dealing with aesthetics, in turn, are designed to function on two levels: either as a subject-by-subject guide to individual product types, or as a continuous narrative chronicling stylistic development. It is thus hoped that the book will function as a handy reference for artists, designers and students, as well as providing historians of the period with a useful addition to the existing literature.

No book of this kind can be compiled without the assistance of a great many people, and in the present instance we are more than usually grateful for the speed, competence and kindness with which museums, galleries and others greeted our requests. In particular, we would like to convey our heartfelt thanks to the following people and institutions who provided us with photographs, information or general encouragement: Joh. Backhausen & Söhne; E. Bakalowits Söhne; Christie, Manson and Woods International, Inc.; Robert Cole; Marianne Feilchenfeldt; Fischer Fine Art, Ltd.; Barry Friedman Ltd. and Jonathan Hallam and Debra Pesci; Gwathmey Siegel & Associates, Architects; Robert Haas (Ram Press); Richard Horn; Peter and Christine Kamm; Knoll International, Inc.; J. & L. Lobmeyr; Richard Meier & Partners; Susan and François de Menil; Galerie Metropol, Inc. and Wolfgang Ritschka; Gallery Modernism and Frank Maraschiello; Lillian Nassau, Ltd. and Arlie M. Sulka; the Cooper-Hewitt Museum, New York; the Metropolitan Museum of Art, New York; the Museum of Modern Art, New York, and Thomas D. Grischkowsky; Swid Powell Design; Eduard F. Sekler; Greta Shapiro; the Shepherd Gallery; Carl Schorske; Unika Vaev/I.C.F., Inc.; Kirk Varnedoe; Peter Vergo; the Historisches Museum der Stadt Wien, Vienna and Hans Bisanz; the Österreichische Galerie, Vienna; the Österreichisches Museum für angewandte Kunst, Vienna and Helga Högl; the Österreichische Nationalbibliothek; Christopher Wilk; Woka/Wolfgang Karolinsky; and a number of private collectors who have requested anonymity. Special thanks must go to the various people who so kindly agreed to be interviewed for this book: Rita Boley-Bolaffio, Charles Gwathmey, Nora Wärndorfer Hodges, Gretl Urban, and especially Mäda Primavesi, the daughter of Otto and Eugenia Primavesi, who in numerous delightful conversations relayed her memories of her parents' years with the Wiener Werkstätte. We are also particularly grateful to James May, who unstintingly put at our disposal his library, his vast collection of Wiener Werkstätte textiles and his equally far-ranging knowledge of the field. Finally, a word of thanks to the staff of the Galerie St. Etienne, which collectively acted as picture researcher, photographer, proofreader and editorial consultant to the project, in particular, to Hildegard Bachert and Margery King, and to Vita Künstler, our representative in Vienna.

8. Josef Hoffmann. Exhibition pavilion for the Kunstschau, Vienna. 1908.

BACKGROUND: IN SEARCH OF THE TOTAL ARTWORK

In 1898 the Vienna Secession, a coalition of relatively progressive painters, architects and designers, opened the doors of its new building, whose dome of gilded leaves, rising above the stalls of the nearby *Naschmarkt*, or vegetable market, soon inspired the nickname "Golden Cabbage" (fig. 9). Ten years later, many of the artists who had originally joined to celebrate the opening of the Secession would reunite in an austere, almost neoclassical building (fig. 8) specially designed by the architect Josef Hoffmann to house an artistic roundup called, quite simply, Kunstschau (Art Show).

In the intervening decade, the participants in these two artistic events had experienced so many stylistic upheavals that one might, under ordinary circumstances, expect them to encompass a lifetime. The ornate Art Nouveau represented by the Secession building's leguminous dome passed quickly with the fading century and was replaced, in the early 1900s, by a geometric severity that, with its emphasis on functionalism and integrity of materials, heralded the coming era of modern architecture and design. The craft-oriented adherents of this avant-garde design mode, dubbed the "Stylists" (*Stilisten*) in opposition to the more traditional painters at the Secession, the "Naturalists" (or *nicht-Stilisten*), formed a loose group whose nucleus, after 1903, was the Wiener Werkstätte (Vienna Workshop). By the time the Stylists, whose conflict with the Naturalists had forced them to leave the Secession in 1905, convened for the 1908 Kunstschau,

9. Josef Maria Olbrich.
Secession building, Vienna;
view of the dome and front
façade. 1898.

Viennese design was undergoing yet another shift, this toward an eclecticism incorporating more fanciful as well as historical and vernacular elements. Ultimately, the most important contribution of the Kunstschau was not this eclecticism, which must be viewed as an essentially reactionary development, but the proto-Expressionistic work of a young newcomer, Oskar Kokoschka. Within ten short years, Viennese design had traveled the tortuous road from Art Nouveau exuberance to the Expressionist apocalypse.

The most talented predecessors of the Expressionist generation were geared not to the fine, but to the applied arts, and so it was that *fin-de-siècle* Viennese culture had its roots in a similarly design-oriented phenomenon, the Biedermeier style of the early nineteenth century. The period that came to be known as Biedermeier (after a fictitious "everyman" of that name) roughly spanned the years between the Napoleonic wars and the revolution of 1848. During these years, the Austrian public, weary of fighting and perhaps already sensing the tensions that would trigger the revolution, immersed itself in family, home and *Kleinkunst* (decorative art or, literally, "little art"). The result was a culture that tended to blur the distinctions generally separating the fine and the applied arts, and many of the popular genre and flower painters of the day also decorated glassware and ceramics. Like the Wiener Werkstätte, the Biedermeier was an invasive design movement that touched every aspect of everyday life, from furniture to fashion, from porcelain to painting. Unlike the Wiener Werkstätte, it possessed no all-encompassing philosophy or moral imperative. Although Biedermeier had as many design ramifications as the Wiener Werkstätte, and likewise produced its share of pure kitsch, it won its place in history for the creation of simple, classically inspired furniture in fruitwood veneers (figs. 10 and 11). It was this furniture that, years later, would be hailed by Hoffmann and Moser as constituting the "last valid tradition," and that they would use to furnish the first small office of the Wiener Werkstätte.

HISTORICISM

In the wake of the 1848 revolution and, more specifically, the destruction, ordered by the Emperor Franz Josef in 1857, of the medieval ramparts that enclosed the inner city, Vienna entered an era of expansion and expansiveness that took its name from the broad, circular boulevard that replaced the old walls: the Ringstrasse. In contrast to the private, inward-looking Biedermeier period, the Ringstrasse era was public and grandiose. The new boulevard required new buildings, and the new buildings, in turn, required decorative murals and frescoes by the score. Artists came from all over Europe to vie for the lucrative commissions. In particular, the Ringstrasse attracted painters of the Romantic movement, many of whom originally studied in Vienna but had long ago abandoned Austria for Germany. Of the younger generation, the most famous painter was Hans Makart, and he, too, gave his name to the period: the *"Makartstil,"* a combination of pompous elegance and lightly veiled sexuality, became the rage. There were "Makart hats" and "Makart bouquets" and

long lines (forty thousand people in five days) whenever a newly completed painting was shown.

The style of the Ringstrasse was blatantly historicist, recalling the past both in architectural quotations and in the allegorical subject matter of its decorative murals. The purpose of all this—to glorify the Habsburg regime and bring prominence to a capital that all too often felt more like a provincial backwater—was an undeniable boon to the city of Vienna. It may even be argued that without the Ringstrasse explosion of the 1860s and 1870s, there would have been no *fin-de-siècle* renaissance, for the artistic and economic support structure would have been lacking. Nonetheless, those artists born during this heady period inherited a legacy of historicism that was burdened with the dead weight of the past to which it was shackled. "It was a very unfavorable time for us young people," Koloman Moser recalled. "Everyone was completely enthralled by the Makart craze with its playful ephemera [*Gschnas*] and its dusty bouquets."[1] Another contemporary observer noted that while the great architects of the Ringstrasse period, such as Heinrich Ferstel, Theophil Hansen and Karl Freiherr von Hasenauer, "were able to thoroughly master the ancient styles without sacrificing their independence, their pupils and imitators, on the other hand, became hopelessly enslaved to those styles."[2] Adolf Loos, an architect whose travels in America had inspired a revolutionary fervor for enlightened design and a loathing for Austrian provincialism, put it far more bluntly in his 1898 essay, "Potemkin's Town." Comparing the Ringstrasse's neo-Baroque and neo-Renaissance apartment buildings, whose cast concrete ornamentation emulated the stucco or stone of genuine palaces, to the canvas and pasteboard village constructed to deceive Catherine the Great, he issued a rallying cry for his generation:

> Not everyone can have been born the lord of a great feudal demesne. We must not be ashamed of the fact that we rent a flat in a building with many other people on the same social level as ourselves. We should not be ashamed of the fact that there are some building materials which are too expensive for us, nor be ashamed of the fact that we live in the nineteenth century and do not want to have a house built in the style of another period. This would be the way to see just how quickly we would be given a style of architecture suited to the times.... I mean a style which can be handed on to posterity with a clear conscience and be singled out with pride even in the distant future.[3]

In bridging the gap between historicism and later developments, the architect Otto Wagner played a crucial role (fig. 13). Although he abandoned historicism—the superficial use of ornament to mimic past styles—he did not abandon historical tradition, remaining firmly convinced that "every new style arises gradually out of the previous one, in that new forms of construction, new materials, new human needs and attitudes link up with the previously existing to produce new creations."[4] He believed that it was the principles of classicism, rather than any particular style, that were worthy of emulation; if these were applied to contemporary needs and circumstances, the result would automatically be a contemporary idiom. "The point of departure of every artistic cre-

10. Biedermeier secretary.
Early 19th century. Mahog-
any. Approximately 6′ high.

11. Biedermeier side chair.
Ca. 1815. Ebonized birch and
fruitwood. Approximately 34″
high.

ation," he wrote, "must be the need, the capacity, the means and the qualities of 'our' time."[5] It is no accident that this man was the esteemed mentor not only of Loos, but of his archrival, Hoffmann. Another of Wagner's influential contributions was his contention that the means of construction must dictate the ultimate form of an architectural structure. Thus the bolts that hold the cladding to the exterior of his *Postsparkasse* (Postal Savings Bank) determine the decorative scheme of the façade (pl. 11), and the aluminum strips that protect the chairs inside the bank from wear double as ornamental embellishments (fig. 12).

THE SECESSION

In 1894 Wagner was appointed head of the architecture department at Vienna's Academy of Fine Art, replacing the more conservative Hasenauer, who had died that year. Among Wagner's students, and soon to become one of his favorite protégés, was Josef Hoffmann, who had come to

Vienna several years earlier after undergoing preliminary technical training in his native Moravia and a one-year apprenticeship in Germany. Wagner's other protégé, three years Hoffmann's senior and already an employee in Wagner's firm, was Josef Maria Olbrich. Olbrich and Hoffmann, together with Koloman Moser (a former student of the Academy's painting department) and four other colleagues, fell into the habit of meeting regularly at the Café Sperl to discuss the burning issues of the day; they called themselves the *Siebener Klub*, or Club of Seven. A similar group, whose members included the painter Carl Moll and the graphic designer Alfred Roller, met at the Café zum Blauen Freihaus and took the name Hagenbund, after the café's proprietor. In the course of the next years, the two groups would mingle under the auspices of the Genossenschaft bildender Künstler Wiens (Vienna Society of Fine Artists), which ran the city's only exhibition facility for contemporary art, the Künstlerhaus.

The Künstlerhaus, sanctioned by the emperor in 1861 and opened nine years later, must be viewed (despite its ultimate historical role) as an essentially progressive innovation. Its function—to represent (for the first time in Vienna) the cause of the living artist and to promote cultural exchanges with other European countries—was not only commendable, it was remarkably similar to that of its eventual antagonist, the Secession. Like the Secession, it had no fixed stylistic program, but its policy of democratic rule fostered a situation in which the conservative majority came to dictate policy. Thus in both the Künstlerhaus and the Secession, there were continual squabbles over committee posts, jury decisions and the selection processes that determined what would be sent to prestigious international exhibitions. The Künstlerhaus, how-

ever, came to seem corrupt because of the manner in which it combined conservativism with commerce. The 10 percent commission garnered on sales of its members' work, it was alleged, caused the Künstlerhaus to favor the work of the retrograde—and presumably more successful—artists.[6] It no longer served its original purpose; its policies seemed hopelessly geared to the preservation of the status quo, and exhibitions of foreign art, while not eliminated entirely, were deliberately held in check to protect the domestic market.

Repeated attempts were made to correct the perceived injustices at the Künstlerhaus, but in 1897, facing censure by the executive committee, the avant-garde felt compelled to

12

13

12. Otto Wagner. Chair designed for the Postsparkasse (Postal Savings Bank). 1904. Stained beechwood with aluminum fittings. 35″ high. Executed by Gebrüder Thonet.

13. Otto Wagner.

14. Otto Wagner. Stool designed for the Postsparkasse (Postal Savings Bank). 1904. Stained beechwood with aluminum fittings. 18½″ high. Executed by Gebrüder Thonet.

14

secede from the parent organization. The painter Gustav Klimt, who had been elected president of the Secession, summed up its intentions as follows: "Our views culminate in the recognition of the necessity of bringing artistic life in Vienna into more lively contact with the continuing development of art abroad, and of putting exhibitions on a purely artistic footing, free from any commercial considerations; of thereby awakening in wider circles a purified, modern view of art; and lastly, of inducing heightened concern for art in official circles."[8] As its motto, the Secession formulated a maxim upon which a broad group of artists, fed up with historicism, could readily agree: "To the age its art, to art its freedom." Beyond this, the Secession endorsed no particular stylistic mode; the issue was not one of style, but rather of quality of life. Unlike the smaller, aesthetically oriented groups that would usher in modernism throughout the rest of Europe (the *Blaue Reiter* and *Brücke* in Germany, Picasso's circle in France), the Secession was principally concerned with controlling and administering the circumstances under which art was created. Foremost among its goals was a plea for "the right to create artistically."[9] To this end, it concocted a program comprising exhibitions of foreign and domestic art, the establishment of a museum of contemporary art,[10] and its own house organ, *Ver Sacrum* (Sacred Spring). Insofar as it was concerned with the sale of its members' work, the Secession was by no means freer of commercial considerations than had been the Künstlerhaus, and it was, in fact, this very problem that triggered the 1905 split between the Stylists and the Naturalists.

From the start, the Secessionists displayed an unusual interest in the applied arts, which had never been incorporated into the exhibition program of the Künstlerhaus. This manifested itself in the type of work shown and in the care lavished on customized installations. "We recognize no difference between high art and low art," the Secessionists declared in *Ver Sacrum*. "All art is good."[11] The groundwork was thus laid for the leveling of fine art and craft that would become one of the guiding principles of the Wiener Werkstätte. The notion of parity between these disparate art forms was, of course, nothing new to Vienna; far more anomalous was the historicist interlude that separated the *fin-de-siècle* crafts movement from its Biedermeier progenitor. The enthusiasm that Makart's paintings aroused, with their large crowds and silly allied fads, was unparalleled in the history of Austrian culture, while a concern with creature comforts—the much-vaunted *Gemütlichkeit* (cosiness)—was as Viennese as whipped cream and chocolate cake. It is therefore not surprising that when Vienna finally awoke from its historicist dream, it was not the painters, but the applied artists who led the way.

For years, the Österreichisches Museum für Kunst und Industrie (Austrian Museum for Art and Industry) had been one of the more energetic arts institutions in the city of Vienna.[12] Founded in 1864 on the model of London's South Kensington Museum,[13] its mission, as its name implied, was to serve as a liaison between art and industry, revitalizing the latter by exposing it to the former. This was accomplished through a multilevel program of educating, collecting, and exhibiting prime examples of the applied arts of all nations and periods. The museum administered the Kunstgewerbeschule (School of Arts and Crafts) founded in 1867 in the capital,[14] as well as a network of technical schools (*Fachschulen*) in the provinces. In addition to exhibiting the objects from its collection, the museum made them available on loan to the technical schools and industries, and set up a drawing studio where selected examples could be copied. Professional craftsmen were encouraged to execute the designs of Kunstgewerbeschule teachers and graduates, with special grants and the possibility of a museum acquisition as extra incentives. Finally, the museum provided a forum for the fruits of its labors in the form of annual winter exhibitions and special commemorative events. Contact with developments abroad was maintained by means of the international expositions that in the nineteenth century provided important, competitive showcases for the latest innovations of the gradually industrializing European nations.

In 1897, the same year that the Secession was founded, Arthur von Scala was named director of the Österreichisches Museum für Kunst und Industrie. A forward-thinking man who had traveled in France and England, Scala immediately brought a breath of fresh air to the museum and was perceived as an ally of the Secession, of which he was a member.[15] At the same time, the Kunstgewerbeschule was restructured so as to give it more autonomy from the museum. A new director, Felician von Myrbach, was appointed, and within a few years he had thoroughly peppered his teaching staff with Secessionists: Roller had been at the school since 1893, Hoffmann joined in 1898, Moser in 1899, and Arthur Strasser, a sculptor, in 1900.[16] The Kunstgewerbeschule thus became, in one fell swoop, the single most important official bastion of the new art movement. The significance of this position became abundantly clear over the course of the next years, as these teachers produced graduates, who in turn became teachers and produced more graduates, casting their influence upon Viennese art and design on into the 1960s, when the last of the teachers associated with the *fin-de-siècle* movement finally retired.[17] The Kunstgewerbeschule also became an important training ground for Wiener Werkstätte employees, fully 80 percent of whom attended the school.

While the Kunstgewerbeschule took the lead in training the up-and-coming members of the avant-garde, the Academy of Fine Arts, with the exception of Otto Wagner, remained a bastion of conservatism. Thus Klimt, the foremost painter of his day, had in the 1870s studied not at the Academy, but at the Kunstgewerbeschule. And in the 1890s Moser, after six years at the Academy, felt compelled to enroll for an additional two years at the Kunstgewerbeschule, where he studied with Klimt's partner, Franz Matsch. Despite Klimt's prominence, his nomination to an Academy professorship was rejected, and likewise, Wagner's suggestion that Hoffmann succeed him was never carried out. As late as 1909, when Egon Schiele was a student at the Academy, his notoriously dictatorial teacher, Christian Griepenkerl, forbade his class to attend the Secession's exhibitions, even though by this time the radical Stylists were long gone.[18] The Academy's almost unilateral rejection of the new movement further contributed to the dominance that the applied arts, through the Kunstgewerbeschule, came to exert.

FOREIGN INFLUENCES

With Scala in charge at the museum, and Myrbach at the Kunstgewerbeschule—both men familiar with design trends outside of Austria—and with the Secession's stated goal of bringing the nation into closer contact with foreign developments, it was natural that the arts and crafts should acquire a more international orientation. Viennese designers, who like the painters had thus far been completely overwhelmed by historicism, were late in adopting the Art Nouveau style that was so influential throughout Western Europe. This style, with its lush flowers and creeping tendrils, never became truly established in Vienna, but rather assumed a transitional status. Instead of endowing decorative forms with botanical or anthropomorphic features, the Viennese endowed anthropomorphic or botanical forms (that is, representational subject matter) with decorative features (figs. 15 and 16). This reversal of the standard Art Nouveau formula stressed the incorporation of geometric motifs for their own sake, and it explains how the Secessionists were able to pass so quickly from the Art Nouveau phase of the 1890s to the severe geometry of the early 1900s.

Of pivotal importance to this development was the Secession's eighth exhibition, a survey of modern European design held in the final months of 1900. Included was representative work by Paris's Maison Moderne, Charles Robert Ashbee's British Guild of Handicrafts, the Belgian designer Henry van de Velde, and the Glasgow "School" of Charles Rennie Mackintosh and Margaret MacDonald. If Ashbee's workshop principle was to provide an important theoretical link in the chain that led to the formation of the Wiener Werkstätte, the contributions of the Glasgow School have long been considered the dominant aesthetic influence. Much can be said on the subject of who influenced whom, and little definitely proven.[19] It is probably most accurate to conclude that the interior designs of Mackintosh and MacDonald were so closely related to trends already taking place in Vienna that an affinity between the two groups developed that led them, for a brief period, to pursue parallel courses. The Glasgow group's geometric handling of forms bore the same inverted relationship to Art Nouveau that the Austrians' did. The use of geometric motifs—in particular, the square—had been pioneered by Mackintosh as early as 1898, but in a manner that was purely decorative.[20] It was only later that both he and Hoffmann evolved an approach wherein furniture construction and rectilinear design became thoroughly integrated (figs. 18 and 19). Other aspects of the room that Mackintosh and MacDonald assembled for the eighth Secession exhibition—the starkness of its black and white color scheme, and the raised frieze (fig. 17)—had a more immediate and obvious influence in Vienna than did the furniture, which had not yet renounced Art Nouveau curves. Although Mackintosh was paraded through Vienna in a wagon of flowers, it must not be assumed that his reception there was entirely enthusiastic. Sales at the Secession exhibition were hardly brisk, and the critical response was lukewarm at best.[21]

Perhaps the closest bond between Mackintosh and the Austrians was their mutual rejection of historical precedent.

Historicism acted as a sharp prod pushing the Secessionists in the direction of the new and untried. Imitation of any sort was anathema to them, and thus they initially sought their models less in established styles than in formal systems and theoretical constructs. When discussion turns to the influence of the British Arts and Crafts movement, mention is often made of the availability of English models through the Secession exhibition, Scala's contacts and such widely read journals as *The Studio* and *Dekorative Kunst*. However, these explanations do not go far enough in elucidating the fascination that the British example held not only for the Austrians, but also for their German colleagues at this time. What the British offered was not so much a style as a system for dealing

15. Koloman Moser. Illustration for *Ver Sacrum*. 1901.

with the aesthetic implications of the looming modern age. England, the first heavily industrialized nation, was also the first to face the resulting problems. This concern may have originated as early as 1836, when the British government prepared a series of comprehensive reports on design and industry, and it found its first philosophical expression in the writings of John Ruskin and William Morris.[22] By the time Hoffmann and his colleagues came on the scene, the English crafts revival was a well-rooted, multigenerational phenomenon that had established significant offshoots in America and Scotland.

To speak of British Arts and Crafts as a single, unified movement is slightly misleading, for as implied above, its vast sweep over time and place engendered a multiplicity of interpretations and concerns, only some of which were of eventual interest to the Austrians. For one thing, the specter of industrialization cast a far less ominous shadow over Austria than it did over Britain. To this day, Austria is not a heavily industrialized nation, and such industry as did exist in the old empire was largely confined to the more distant provinces, in what are now Hungary and Czechoslovakia. While certain products were manufactured by enterprises classified as "factories" (as it expanded, the Wiener Werkstätte would also acquire "factory" status), the designation is misleading, for it refers to the size of the operation rather than to the method of production. "Factories" were often no more than large organizations of craftsmen, who, while delegating minor tasks to subordinates, supervised the construction of each item from start to finish. Assembly-line production was unusual, especially for the more luxurious sort of domestic accouterments, such as furniture, that interested the Wiener Werkstätte.

The relative lack of industrialization in Austria meant that the social programs of the British movement, which were designed to salvage the lower classes from their miserable working conditions, had less relevance. Austria's social problems were of a different nature, and could not be addressed

designs in the nation's "factories," unlike the Germans, they did not allow the requirements of modern industrial production to shape their creative solutions. The British crafts imperative, which had been admired but never strictly followed, conspired with the Austrian industrial environment to cripple the growth of the Werkstätte enterprise.

One of the happy paradoxes of the British Arts and Crafts movement was that this essentially reactionary effort, which hoped to stem the tide of industrialization by returning to the values of a purer time (specifically, the Middle Ages), provided the impetus, in Austria and Germany, for the modern design trend that culminated with the Bauhaus in Dessau. In this respect, the Wiener Werkstätte forms a decisive link between the British movement and all that came later. Many aspects of the Bauhaus's work program recalled crafts ideals similar to those of the Werkstätte. "The Bauhaus," stated the program, "wants to educate architects, painters and sculptors to all levels, according to their capabilities, to become competent craftsmen or independent creative artists and to form a community of leading and future artist craftsmen."[25] The Austrian movement's regard for craftsmanship, with its correlative interest in the physical construction of objects, pro-

16

16. Mileva Stoisavljevic. Decorative border. Ca. 1903–04. Color lithograph. Published in *Die Fläche*.

logically by a progressive cultural program. The system against which the Secessionists revolted was primarily aesthetic, and the revolt itself (despite a token effort to educate the working classes through special exhibition tours with reduced admission fees) was almost completely apolitical. If asked, most of the Secessionists would probably have echoed Hoffmann's contention that political problems were better left to the politicians.[23] Few of these so-called revolutionary artists were in any sense political revolutionaries, as is confirmed by the fact that such "radicals" as Loos, Schoenberg and Schiele all supported the aristocracy.[24] The second important implication of Austria's industrial backwardness was that it necessarily limited the long-term impact of the Wiener Werkstätte. While Hoffmann and Moser initially found a very congenial response to their craft-oriented

vided a model that remained valid well into the twentieth century. The oft-repeated maxim of the American architect Louis Sullivan, "Form follows function," proceeded from the demand for integrity in the use of materials and in overall design that was, in turn, a natural outgrowth of the crafts ethic. One had only to substitute, for the revered and outmoded craftsman, the new and powerful machine to come up with an art that, instead of being subverted by industrialization, would accept it as a tool and bridge to the next era.

The final legacy that the British crafts movement left its Austrian heirs was the tendency to apply its standards across the board or, as stated in the manifesto of Arthur Mackmurdo's Century Guild, "to render all branches of art the sphere no longer of the tradesman, but of the artist."[26] While all the groups that were included in the eighth Secession exhibition shared this desire to reaestheticize the objects of everyday use, none would carry the principle as far as the Wiener Werkstätte, whose efforts touched such diverse areas as fashion, publishing and stage design as well as architecture and interior decoration. Not only did the Wiener Werkstätte embrace every field of creative endeavor (sometimes without any prior experience or expertise) but it demanded of its collaborators a concomitant flexibility of vocation. "Either one is an artist," Olbrich believed, "and then one must be able to do everything, or one is merely a technician who has mastered a particular craft."[27] Hoffmann and Moser were undoubtedly the most talented and versatile in the group, but most of the Wiener Werkstätte artists were active in several areas; if they attended the Kunstgewerbeschule, this was part of their training.

THE AUSTRIAN GESAMTKUNSTWERK

The philosophical underpinning of the Wiener Werkstätte's great variety of activities was the principle of the *Gesamtkunstwerk*, or total artwork: the integration of all the various design elements in a single aesthetic environment. Like the British Arts and Crafts movement, the *Gesamtkunstwerk* was a mid-nineteenth-century innovation that proved particularly adaptable to early-twentieth-century requirements long after the specific forms that it had originally called forth had passed from currency. It was also remarkably flexible, turning up now in music, then in painting or architecture and finally, in Hitler's totalitarian regime—the ultimate *Gesamtkunstwerk*. The composer Richard Wagner is generally credited with formulating the concept, if not the term, in a series of publications written between 1849 and 1851.[28] Opera, with its unique combination of music, theater, dance, literature and decorative arts, provided the perfect model for the *Gesamtkunstwerk*, but the idea can easily be traced back to the Romantic movement's early interest in the reunification of art and architecture through the revival of classical fresco technique and mural painting. From this latter approach, which informed much Ringstrasse design, came the Wiener Werkstätte's interpretation of the *Gesamtkunstwerk* as a comprehensive treatment of architectural space, which in a manner analogous to opera incorporates a host of subsidiary art forms. The Viennese version of the concept found its final flowering in the work program of the Bauhaus, whose stated goal was "to bring together all creative effort into one whole, to reunify all disciplines of practical art—sculpture, painting, handicrafts and the crafts—as inseparable components of a new architecture. The ultimate, if distant, aim of the Bauhaus is the unified work of art—the great structure—in which there is no distinction between monumental and decorative art."[29]

The notion of the *Gesamtkunstwerk* as it applied to *fin-de-siècle* Austrian design was a conjunction of the rather lofty Germanic interpretation of that same concept, as exemplified by Wagnerian opera, and the down-to-earth British crafts movement. These seemingly disparate entities found their logical point of communion in a nation that, with its legendary frivolity and love of festivity, gave new meaning to the line "All the world's a stage." In the transformation of art into theater, Makart had no rival, and his paintings, ensconced in elegant buildings that were hardly more than neo-Renaissance or Baroque frames, provided the perfect stage setting for the fantasy of imperial power that was then being enacted in Vienna. It is fitting that Makart was best remembered not for his crowd-pleasing paintings, but for the orchestration of a mammoth parade, or *Festzug*, held to commemorate the emperor's twenty-fifth wedding anniversary in 1879. Such ceremonies, typical of Vienna's historical love of spectacle, opera and theatrical entertainment, encouraged a participatory loss of identity that for the moment eclipsed the realities of ordinary life. This blurring of the boundaries that normally separate life from art, coupled with an ingrained propensity to merge "high" art and "low," paved the way for the characteristically Viennese interpretation of the *Gesamtkunstwerk* as everyday environment.[30]

Thus it was that the *Gesamtkunstwerk* concept, which had been created for the stage, entered the home, and the home, as a result, became a stage, subject to the whims of its architect/impresario. "Everything in a room must be like an instrument in an orchestra," wrote Hermann Bahr, "the architect is the conductor, the whole should produce a symphony."[31] It was literally forbidden to move any object in a Hoffmann-designed room from its prescribed place, as the Swiss painter Ferdinand Hodler learned when, on a visit to Vienna, he tried this and was immediately corrected by a well-trained servant. Such dogmatism was satirized in Loos's essay about a "Poor Rich Man" who is tyrannized by his architect. The rich man calls in the architect to consult about any proposed change, however minor, in his home, and quakes with fear when the architect glowers at his slippers:

The rich man looked at his embroidered slippers and breathed a sigh of relief, for this time he was entirely innocent. The slippers had been made after an original design by the architect himself. So he retorted, "My dear architect! Surely you haven't forgotten? You designed these slippers yourself."

"Certainly I did," thundered the architect. "But I designed them for the bedroom. In this room you ruin the whole atmosphere with those two ghastly patches of color. Can't you see?"[32]

Loos' story about the slippers has an ironic counterpart in reality. Supposedly Eduard Wimmer-Wisgrill, on a visit to the lavish mansion that the Wiener Werkstätte had designed for the Stoclet family in Brussels, was appalled by the fact that Madame Stoclet's Paris fashions clashed with the decor. The solution seemed obvious: on his return to Vienna, Wimmer set up a fashion department for the Wiener Werkstätte.[33]

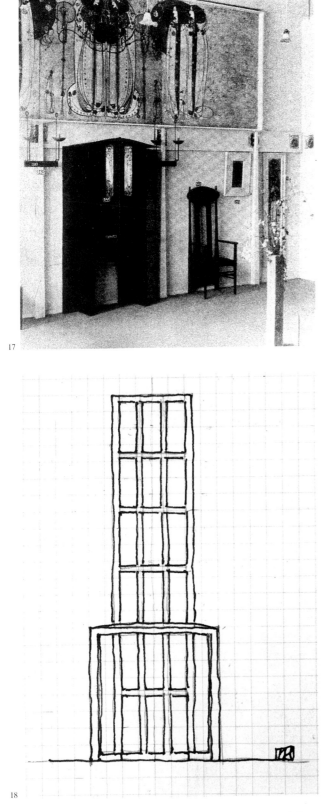

17

18

17. Charles Rennie Mackintosh. Room designed for the eighth Secession exhibition. 1900.

18. Josef Hoffmann. Sketch for a high-backed chair. 1903. Pencil and blue pen on graph paper. Initialed, lower right. 8⅜″ × 11¾″.

19. Charles Rennie Mackintosh. High-backed ladder-back chair. 1902. Ebonized wood. 55¼″ high.

19

20. Josef Hoffmann and
Koloman Moser. Entrance to
the Wiener Werkstätte exhibition at the Hohenzollern
Kunstgewerbehaus, Berlin.
1904.

A BRIEF HISTORY
OF THE WIENER WERKSTÄTTE

The positions occupied by Josef Hoffmann and Koloman Moser at the Secession and the Kunstgewerbeschule provided them with important tools for publicizing and propagating their ideas. Through exhibitions they could reach the public, and through their teaching they could direct the development of the next generation of artists. What they lacked, however, was control over the means of production and sale of their work. Designers, unlike painters, generally require craftsmen to assist in the execution of their efforts, and sporadic exhibitions at a fine-arts oriented institution such as the Secession are not as effective in producing income as a permanent sales outlet or, better still, a steady stream of commissions. The Wiener Werkstätte, like the Secession before it, was principally a means for artists to gain command over the circumstances of creation.

Like the Secession, it had no stylistic program as such, but rather was organized according to broad theoretical precepts. Over the course of its near thirty-year history, it passed through numerous stylistic phases. This flexibility in the face of changing tastes was one of the reasons for its relative longevity. The Werkstätte's demise, on the other hand, was triggered in part by an equal inflexibility when it came to modifying its underlying principles.

21

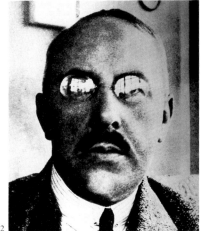

22

23

21. Koloman Moser.

22. Josef Hoffmann.

23. Fritz Wärndorfer.

Viennese artistic circles in the early twentieth century were unusually concerned with the exhibition, promotion and sale of their own work. Whereas in other European countries Secession movements were dying out and being replaced by a more modern system of dealers and other artistic middlemen, in Vienna direct contact between artists and their patrons remained the rule rather than the exception.[1] Miethke, the most active commercial gallery, after 1904 was run by a painter, the Secessionist Carl Moll, and as such was more like an arm of the Secession than an independent business.[2] Moll left Miethke in 1912 without having substantially altered the Viennese art scene. Of the next generation, both Kokoschka and Schiele found it necessary to go to Germany for their first serious gallery representation: Kokoschka with the Cassirers and Herwarth Walden in Berlin, Schiele with Hans Goltz in Munich. Kokoschka, despairing of ever finding a friendly reception for his work in Vienna, remained happily in Germany for many years, while Schiele developed a network of complex but not unremunerative relationships with Austrian collectors.

With the passing of the Ringstrasse era and the aging of the emperor, the government severely curtailed its sponsorship of public commissions. The last Ringstrasse commission of note—Klimt's cycle of allegories on the faculties of medicine, jurisprudence, and philosophy for the University of Vienna (fig. 25)—ended in a scandal so intense and sustained that it must have raised serious doubts about the overall future of this sort of public painting. The three allegories, which literally presented their subjects naked, without the protective cloak of historical allusion to which people were accustomed, presaged a concern with personal and psychological values that would resurface in the work of the Expressionists. The university commission, which Klimt had received in 1898, dragged on for years, as each picture in turn was finished, exhibited and reviled by the press and public, until finally, in 1905, Klimt washed his hands of the entire matter by determining to pay back his honorarium and reclaim the works.[3] Thereafter, he received no more such commissions. A fleeting hope that the Christian Socialist mayor of Vienna, Karl Lueger, would step in to replace the emperor as chief patron of the arts was raised when the City of Vienna donated the land for the Secession's building. However, this hope was soon dashed by the Secessionists' essentially apolitical stance and the growing impression that the new art was nothing but an incomprehensible amusement for wealthy aesthetes. The modern style was appropriate for neither the glorification of the aristocratic regime nor the sustenance of the slowly rising masses. Instead, artists turned to the recently established upper middle class, and private sponsorship became the norm for commissions in both architecture and painting.

Without access to an effective system of commercial galleries or a supportive program of government commissions, fin-de-siècle Viennese artists were forced to organize institutions such as the Secession and the Wiener Werkstätte to procure the private patronage that had become indispensable. Though these institutions were ostensibly intended to vouchsafe their members' creative freedom and protect them from the coarser realities of commerce, the fact that they were concerned with the sale as well as the presentation of art constituted an inherent contradiction that eventually destroyed them. In effect, the problems of the Secession and the Wiener Werkstätte mirrored one another, for while the former was an artists' organization beset with commercial conflicts, the latter was a business enterprise handicapped by artistic principles.

An ongoing dispute between the crafts-oriented Stylists and the conventional easel painters, the Naturalists, was brought to a head by Klimt's proposal in 1905 that the Secession purchase the Galerie Miethke. Carl Moll had already been forced to resign from the Secession because of an alleged conflict of interest. The suggestion that the Secession itself, always a de facto dealer for its members, should make a forthright entrance into the commercial sphere revived all the old Künstlerhaus arguments that had led to the formation of the Secession in the first place. In a narrow vote, the naïve if laudable principle of "pure" art won out over the attempt to establish a more realistic vehicle for maintaining contact

24

24. Gustav Klimt. 1908.   25. Gustav Klimt. *Philosophy*. 1899-1907. Oil on canvas. 169¼" × 118⅛".

with the buying public. The result of this election—the en masse resignation of the Stylists or *Klimtgruppe*—left the Secession without its most talented members and these members without an exhibition space. In the years that followed, the only noteworthy exhibitions of contemporary art (with the exception of the two Kunstschauen of 1908 and 1909) were those organized by Miethke and the Wiener Werkstätte. The turn to these two more overtly commercial institutions may be considered a step in the process of securing an economic support system for the production of art. That this development was just a phase, rather than an end in itself, is amply illustrated by the turbulent rise and fall of the Wiener Werkstätte.

26. Josef Diveky. Steinhof Church, Vienna. Color lithograph postcard (No. 405). 3½″ × 5½″. Published by the Wiener Werkstätte.

THE RISE

The Wiener Werkstätte was founded in 1903 by Josef Hoffmann, Koloman Moser and Fritz Wärndorfer.[4] While the precipitous decision is often made to sound as casual as a coffeehouse conversation (which is, according to several firsthand accounts, how the idea originated[5]), the groundwork had certainly been well prepared in advance. The journalist Hermann Bahr had suggested something of the kind as early as 1899: "What is missing is a great organization to link art and craftsmanship.... Let there be a bridge! These two must meet at long last. A tremendous studio, a colony of workshops where the artists will work with the craftsmen, teaching them and learning from them, craftsmanship growing from art, art from craftsmanship."[6] In 1900 the German writer Julius Meier-Graefe seconded the idea when he met Moser and Hoffmann at the Paris World's Fair, and the following year, members of Hoffmann's and Moser's first class of Kunstgewerbeschule graduates took the first tentative step by forming a loose coalition called *Wiener Kunst im Hause* (Viennese Domestic Art).[7] The group exhibited sporadically under the auspices of larger institutions, such as the Wiener Kunstgewerbeverein (Viennese Arts and Crafts Association, in 1901), the Secession (1902), and the annual winter exhibition of the Österreichisches Museum für Kunst und Industrie (1909/10). Foreign models for the Werkstätte

enterprise were provided not only by Ashbee's British Guild of Handicrafts (which Hoffmann visited in 1902), but by German organizations such as the Vereinigte Werkstätten für Kunst und Handwerk (United Workshops for Art and Crafts), founded in 1897, whose members included Peter Behrens and Hermann Obrist, and the Dresdner Werkstätte für Handwerkkunst (Dresden Crafts Workshop), founded in 1898 under the direction of Karl Schmidt.

To the artistic brew that was fermenting at the time, Fritz Wärndorfer provided the key missing ingredient: money. A member of the second generation of a family of prosperous textile manufacturers, he was far less interested in administering the firm's factories in Bohemia and Lower Austria than in dispensing the wealth that emanated therefrom.[8] He had been an enthusiastic supporter of the Secession from the beginning, and in fact met Hoffmann in 1898 on the scaffolding of its rising building. He took a particular interest in the arts and crafts, commissioning a music room from Mackintosh after the Secession's eighth exhibition. Business contacts and frequent trips to England helped him keep alive the contact with the crafts movement there.[9] As plans for the Wiener Werkstätte began to take a more concrete shape, he consulted Mackintosh for advice and, after receiving the Scotsman's blessing, threw himself completely into the enterprise, devoting the greater part of his time and, eventually, his fortune to it.[10]

The work program of the Wiener Werkstätte—formally published only in 1905 but undoubtedly formulated much earlier—was in its essence far less original than the actual work that the Werkstätte produced. Certain notions were clearly derived from the various British crafts organizations, and in fact it was the specified intention of the Werkstätte to follow in the footsteps of Morris and Ruskin. "We wish," stated Hoffmann and Moser, the authors of this manifesto, "to establish intimate contact between public, designer and craftsman, and to produce good, simple domestic requisites. We start from the purpose in hand, usefulness is our first requirement, and our strength has to lie in good proportions and materials well handled."[11] Other goals set forth in the work program, such as the leveling of the fine and the applied arts and the creation of an art appropriate to the age, were warmed over from the early days of the Secession. "The work of the art craftsman is to be measured by the same yardstick as that of the painter and the sculptor," Hoffmann and Moser declared. "So long as our cities, our houses, our rooms, our furniture, our effects, our clothes and our jewelry, so long as our language and feelings fail to reflect the spirit of our times in a plain, simple and beautiful way, we shall be infinitely behind our ancestors." In their proposed invasion not only of art, but of life itself, the founders of the Wiener Werkstätte evoked the spirit of the *Gesamtkunstwerk*, which they merged with the other concepts to create a new and powerful focus for their enterprise. Singly, the ideas of the Wiener Werkstätte were nothing special; together, they were explosive.

The Wiener Werkstätte, which at first had been housed in a provisional three-room apartment, moved in October 1903 to a commodious three-story building on the Neustiftgasse, in Vienna's Seventh District. Here, everything was arranged according to the most modern standards; the press, at the time, was particularly impressed by the indoor plumbing. The white, airy rooms were designed to create a feeling of light and cleanliness; camaraderie among the workers was encouraged, foul language prohibited. The new premises contained facilities for gold, silver, and metalwork, bookbinding, leatherwork, cabinetry[12] and a paint shop, each identifiable by its own color, which was used to code everything from the rooms themselves to the ledgers. Hoffmann merged his architectural practice with the Werkstätte, and for the first year or so of organizational preparation, the new concern executed mainly commissioned work. By 1904, however, they were ready to go public, at an exhibition in Berlin's Hohenzollern Kunstgewerbehaus (Hohenzollern Arts and Crafts House) (fig. 20). For this occasion, the German journal *Deutsche Kunst und Dekoration* (German Art and Decor), which was to develop something of an exclusive relationship with the Wiener Werkstätte, published the first article on the venture. Also in 1904, the Werkstätte received its first major official commission: the creation of a special publication (including graphics, illustrations, typography and binding) to commemorate the hundredth anniversary of the K. und K. Hof und Staatsdruckerei (Imperial and Royal Court and State Printing Press). The fledgling enterprise was on its way.

During the first years of the Wiener Werkstätte's existence, its activities were tightly intertwined with Hoffmann's

architectural commissions, and the collaboration between Hoffmann and Moser remained close—so close, in fact, that in many cases it is impossible to make definite attributions. However, as the Werkstätte grew, Hoffmann and Moser began to pull apart. Moser became more involved with assignments that were essentially solo operations, such as the design of stamps and banknotes for the government, or the altarpiece and stained-glass windows for Otto Wagner's church at the Steinhof mental institution (fig. 26). Preoccupied with the Steinhof commission, which he received in 1904, Moser contributed hardly anything to the Wiener Werkstätte's most collosal undertaking ever, the Stoclet mansion in Brussels[13] (frontispiece, figs. 58 and 59). In 1907 he would leave the Werkstätte entirely. Meanwhile, the Wiener Werkstätte continued to participate in exhibitions, at Miethke and at the Moravian Crafts Museum in 1905, and at the Folkwang Museum in Hagen, Germany, and Earl's Court in London in 1906. Also in 1906, it began to be included regularly in the various officially sponsored international trade expositions, and it opened a new salesroom in its Neustiftgasse building. The following year, the Werkstätte established another sales branch in the center of town, on the fashionable Graben. The expansion of its retail operation was perhaps an inevitable concomitant of growth, and this tendency was furthered by a gradual decrease in the number of comprehensive architectural commissions. As a result of a lawsuit over the accounting for the Wiener Werkstätte's first important commission, the Purkersdorf Sanatorium (completed between 1904 and 1905) (figs. 49-55), Hoffmann withdrew his architectural practice from the firm. He still availed himself of the services of the Werkstätte in outfitting his interiors, and designed showrooms and exhibition installations for the enterprise, but nonetheless, a definite shift in direction had occurred.

In the years after 1910, retail outlets played an increasingly important role in the Wiener Werkstätte's activities and were closely tied to the enlargement of the workshop operation as well. The fashion department, for example, made its debut at the Werkstätte's Karlsbad branch around 1910 and was then formally introduced to Vienna the following year. Originally incorporated in the Neustiftgasse building, the fashion division was given its own headquarters next door to the Graben salesroom in 1911, and by 1914 it had expanded to the point that it was upgraded to "factory" status and required separate production facilities on the Johannesgasse. A pair of showrooms for fashion and textiles were constructed opposite one another on the Kärntnerstrasse, at the heart of Vienna's elegant First District, in 1916 and 1917 respectively. Textile production and ceramics, like fashion design, were not part of the Werkstätte's original program, but were added one by one over the course of the years. By 1928, when the Wiener Werkstätte celebrated its twenty-fifth anniversary with due pomp and ceremony, it could boast arrangements for the production of silver, gold, metal, sheet metal, enamel, leatherwork, bookbinding, fashion, knitwear, beadwork, embroidery, woven, printed and painted fabric, ceramics, carpets, wallpaper, and lacework.[14] As the Werkstätte grew at home, branches in other cities also were added: in Marienbad and Zürich in 1917 (fig. 28), New York in

27. Josef Hoffmann and
Koloman Moser. Reception
room for the Wiener Werk-
stätte's main office on the
Neustiftgasse. 1903–04.

28. Dagobert Peche. Show-
room for the Wiener Werk-
stätte's Zürich branch. 1917.

29. Josef Urban. Showroom
for the Wiener Werkstätte's
New York branch. Ca. 1922.

1921[15] (fig. 29), Velden in 1922, and Berlin in 1929.

Throughout this period, exhibitions served an auxiliary function in promoting the Werkstätte's products. Among the major presentations to which the Wiener Werkstätte contributed were the 1908 and 1909 Kunstschauen in Vienna, and the 1911 international exposition in Rome, for which Hoffmann designed the Austrian pavilion. In 1912 the Deutscher Werkbund, a German union of artists, craftsmen and industry that the Wiener Werkstätte had helped found in 1907, held its annual exhibition at the Museum für Kunst und Industrie in Vienna. This led to the formation of an independent offshoot, the Österreichischer Werkbund,[16] which experienced its finest hour at an exposition sponsored by the Deutscher Werkbund in Cologne in 1914 (fig. 61). Hoffmann again designed the Austrian pavilion for the Cologne exhibi-

tion, which provided the last significant international exposure for the Wiener Werkstätte before World War I. During the first years of the war, international expositions were of necessity severely curtailed, but as the war dragged to a close, exhibitions in neutral countries such as Sweden (1916) and Switzerland (1917) began to be organized, perhaps in a halfhearted attempt to return to normalcy. After the war, exhibition opportunities increased: the Wiener Werkstätte participated in the 1920 Kunstschau in Vienna, and in the 1925 Paris "Exposition internationale des arts décoratifs et industriels modernes," which gave birth to the term "Art Deco." In addition to special presentations, there was the regular run of international trade expositions that, coupled with a steady stream of press coverage, served to keep the Wiener Werkstätte before the public eye.

The multifaceted undertakings of the Wiener Werkstätte—exhibitions at home and abroad, foreign and domestic sales branches—were very naturally reflected in the organization of the workshops themselves. By 1905, when the Wiener Werkstätte published its first modest catalogue containing the Hoffmann/Moser work program, it was said to employ one hundred workers, including thirty-seven master craftsmen. In addition to this permanent staff, the Wiener Werkstätte had loose ties with a number of outside workshops whose products it sold in its salesrooms or incorporated in outside commissions. Around 1907, the Werkstätte took over distribution for the Wiener Keramik, a ceramics studio founded by Berthold Löffler and Michael Powolny in 1906.[17] Both the Wiener Keramik and Leopold Forstner's independent mosaic workshop were employed in connection with the Stoclet project, and the Wiener Keramik also did the colorful wall tiles for the Cabaret Fledermaus in 1907 (pl. 7). Ambiguous relationships with outside artisans characterized the Wiener Werkstätte throughout its history, and it is often impossible to determine who was a regular employee, who a free-lancer, or how such individuals were compensated. In some cases it appears that artisans were hired for specific tasks, in others that they were paid by the piece or through a consignment arrangement. Sometimes the Wiener Werkstätte sent its designs to outside firms for execution; at other times it executed designs purchased from outside artists. A form of cottage industry proved especially efficient for the manufacture of little fabric flowers and other fashion accessories. Another source of collaborators was the Kunstgewerbeschule, which from the start had an informal but self-understood relationship with the Werkstätte. In 1913 Hoffmann established the Artists' Workshops as a forum for experimentation, in effect extending the conditions that existed at the Kunstgewerbeschule beyond the moment of graduation.[18] Artists would receive all supplies gratis, courtesy of the Wiener Werkstätte, but would be compensated for their efforts only if the results were chosen to be sold or produced. By these various means, the Wiener Werkstätte created an enormous network of allied artisans and artists, some two hundred of whom have been identified to date.

As a factory-size group of craftsmen, the Wiener Werkstätte was trapped somewhere between a genuine pure crafts aesthetic and the industrial age. Its characteristic ambivalence toward the machine is already apparent in the work program. "The immeasurable harm caused in the realm of arts and crafts by shoddy mass production, on the one hand, and mindless imitation of old styles on the other, has swept through the entire world like a huge flood," the statement begins. However, it concludes by admitting that "a mass-produced object of tolerable kind can be provided by means of the machine; it must, however, bear the imprint of its manufacture. We do not regard it as our task to enter upon this area as yet."[19] Later industrial design would not only "bear the imprint" of the machine, but consciously incorporate that "imprint" as an integral component of its aesthetic, and it is significant that Hoffmann and Moser already theoretically anticipated this development. Theory and practice, of course, are two different things, and it is evident that the Viennese never considered this a serious option, even though

CHANDELIERS DESIGNED BY F A M O U S A R T I S T S SILVER, BRASS DULL METAL

UNUSAL LAMPS IN BRASS SILVER AND WOOD

BEAUTIFUL SILK SHADES

SILVER LAMP

BY PECHÉ

SILVER MIRROR
SILVER VASES

BY STRNAD
BY HOFMANN

SILVER SERVICE

DESIGN BY PECHÉ

30

30. Two pages from the catalogue of the New York branch, illustrating objects by Dagobert Peche, Oskar Strnad and Josef Hoffmann. Ca. 1922.

31. Wiener Werkstätte after-
noon dress. Hand-printed
China silk. Friederike Maria
Beer had the harem ensemble
worn by her in the Klimt portrait remade into this dress.

32. Gustav Klimt. *Portrait of
Friederike Maria Beer.* 1916.
Oil on canvas. Signed, lower
left. 66⅛″ × 51⅛″.

Mackintosh had suggested that they might eventually progress to "attack the factory on its own ground, and [produce]
objects of use in magnificent form and at such a price that
they lie within the buying range of the poorest."[20]

The Wiener Werkstätte did not by any means shun the
use of machinery. In an early article on the workshops, *Deutsche Kunst und Dekoration* noted that they were "fully
equipped with all the technical innovations that can serve the
enterprise." However, the article continues, "Here the
machine is no ruler or tyrant, but a willing servant and
helper."[21] Hoffmann and Moser had licensed their designs to
outside manufacturers prior to founding the Werkstätte, and
they continued to do so thereafter. For use by its artisans,
the Werkstätte purchased some prefabricated materials, and
it sent out partially completed products to be finished by
machine. Still, the Wiener Werkstätte refused to embrace
industrial production wholeheartedly, for such a position,
taken to its logical conclusion, would require abandoning the
crafts ethic entirely. This became an especially tense issue

after World War I, when the impact of industrialization
began to be felt much more decisively in the area of avant-
garde design. Hoffmann, whose initial views on the subject
were fairly broad-minded, took an increasingly reactionary
stance. Germany and Austria came to represent two opposite
poles: the one urban and geared to mass production, the
other predominantly rural and geared to life on a smaller,
more human scale. Withal, the Wiener Werkstätte plodded
meticulously onward, continuing to craft unique items that
were both costly and impractical. Philipp Häusler, a forward-
thinking administrative director hired by the Wiener Werkstätte in the early 1920s, fell out with Hoffmann over his
attempts to boost the Werkstätte's income by expanding its
program of industrial licenses. "When our things are on view
in every shop on the Mariahilferstrasse [Vienna's main middle-class shopping street]," snorted Hoffmann, "it will all be
up with us."[22]

From its inception, the Wiener Werkstätte had recognized
that industrialization was the wave of the future, and that "it
would be madness to swim against this current."[23] Given the
fact that the Viennese knowingly set out to buck this trend,
it may at first glance seem paradoxical that they nonetheless

33. Friederike Maria Beer in
Wiener Werkstätte dress and
jewelry; sofa by Josef
Hoffmann.

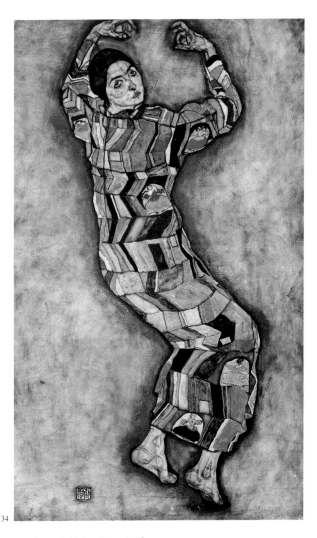

34. Egon Schiele. *Portrait of
Miss Beer.* 1914. Oil on canvas. Signed and dated, lower
left. 74¾″ × 47½″.

viewed themselves as realists. "We are in no position to chase after daydreams," they insisted. "We stand with both feet firmly planted in reality and need tasks to carry out."[24] The truth is that for its time and place, the program of the Wiener Werkstätte *was* realistic. The ready reception of its designs by Austrian industry is evidence of a willingness, or even a need, to embrace a new style. Within a few years of the founding of the Secession, industry paid the movement the highest form of flattery: it copied and, in the process, totally botched up the innovative designs. By 1900, Hermann Bahr was griping about a "false Secession,"[25] and one of the primary purposes of the Wiener Werkstätte was to combat this trend. The Wiener Werkstätte was geared to deal with the industrial situation as it existed in early twentieth century Austria but not to change with it.

THE FALL

Similarly, the financial structure of the Wiener Werkstätte was designed to take advantage of the peculiar socioeconomic circumstances that characterized Vienna at the turn of the century. It grew out of the flow of private patronage that had been stimulated by the Secession and was destroyed, gradually, as the sources of that patronage were cut off. As the imperial and municipal governments abdicated their responsibilities as patrons of the arts, the *haute bourgeoisie* stepped eagerly into the breach. These were the children of the Ringstrasse, a generation grown accustomed to taking an enthusiastic interest in art but weary of Makart and quite ready for something different. While the majority retained their loyalty to historicism—and the nobility had never gotten beyond the Baroque period —the Jewish upper middle class proved most receptive to the innovations of the Secession and the Wiener Werkstätte. Capitalists who wanted to mimic aristocrats, these men and their wives hoped to confirm their newly achieved status by dabbling in artistic patronage—the pleasure of kings. The beneficiaries of enormous, often inherited, wealth, such individuals did not have to labor hard, but only had to oversee their various properties. The rest of their time (which was considerable) and money (equally considerable) they gave wholeheartedly to sport and culture. Involvement with the arts became, for these people, an all-consuming passion. The idea, explains Mäda Primavesi, daughter of one of the Wiener Werkstätte's chief backers, "was not just to buy paintings or sculptures, but to live the life, humanly, intellectually, socially."[26]

Thus when the Wiener Werkstätte was first established, it found itself with a small ready-made nucleus of patrons. Karl Wittgenstein, who had put up 120,000 kronen[27] toward the Secession's building, became one of Hoffmann's most important early clients. Hoffmann designed two administrative buildings in Lower Austria (where Wittgenstein owned forests) for him in 1900 and redecorated his Hochreith hunting lodge, also in Lower Austria, in 1906 (fig. 57). Wittgenstein's daughter, Margaret Stonborough, had her Berlin apartment done by Hoffmann and Moser in 1905. The journalist Bertha Zuckerkandl, one of the most vociferous champions of the Secession, persuaded her brother-in-law Viktor to give the Wiener Werkstätte the important but ill-fated Purkersdorf Sanatorium job. The overlap between patrons of the fine and of the applied arts is amply demonstrated by Klimt's roster of sitters. Not only Margaret Stonborough-Wittgenstein, but Friederike Maria Beer (fig. 32), Marie Henneberg, Sonja Knips, Serena Lederer, Magda Mautner-Markhof,[28] Eugenia (pl. 6) and Mäda Primavesi (fig. 39), all had direct connections with the Wiener Werkstätte and/or Hoffmann.

Friederike Maria Beer was undoubtedly one of the most zealous of the Werkstätte's clients (fig. 33). By her own admission "a walking advertisement for the Wiener Werkstätte," she recalled, "I was so wild about the Wiener Werkstätte that every stitch of clothing I owned was designed by them. When I got an apartment of my own, all the furniture, even the rugs, was made by them."[29] She has also won her place in history as the only person to be painted by both Klimt and Schiele (and one of Schiele's few female portrait sitters). Apparently each artist had difficulty coming to terms with the flamboyant patterns of Fräulein Beer's Wiener Werkstätte clothing; Klimt, in the end, asked her to turn the jacket inside out, and Schiele strewed South American straw dolls all over her recumbent body. She was able to pay for the Schiele portrait herself (fig. 34). The Klimt portrait, at 34,000 kronen (then roughly $7,000), was a gift from her artist friend Hans Böhler; she had a choice between that or a string of pearls.[30]

Friederike Maria Beer can hardly be considered a "typical" Wiener Werkstätte client, for the average customer surely did not buy in such overwhelming quantities, but her artistic associations are not at all atypical. Next to the upper middle class, the most important single support group of the Wiener Werkstätte was the artistic community itself. Hoffmann's first major commission was a series of villas for four of his fellow Secessionists—Carl Moll, Koloman Moser, Hugo Henneberg and Friedrich Spitzer—built on Vienna's Hohe Warte between 1900 and 1902. Prior to this, he had designed furnishings for Moser and the artists Max Kurzweil and Fernand Khnopff. Close relationships between Hoffmann and artists continued after the founding of the Wiener Werkstätte. (It was, in fact, the sculptor Anton Hanak who introduced the architect to one of the Werkstätte's most important patrons, Otto Primavesi.) Among the Werkstätte's commissions were the fashion salon for Klimt's lover, Emilie Flöge (fig. 36), and furniture for Klimt himself, for Carl Otto Czeschka, Hans Böhler, Ferdinand Hodler (fig. 35), and for

35

35. Josef Hoffmann. Dining chair, mirror and sideboard designed for Ferdinand Hodler. Ca. 1913–14. Gray polished oak, with fabric by Dagobert Peche.

36. Josef Hoffmann and Koloman Moser. Flöge Sisters clothing salon, Vienna; reception room. 1904.

Broncia and Hugo Koller.

A fair number of the Wiener Werkstätte's main clients were also its backers or artists, and sometimes, when they failed to pay their bills, they were creditors and debtors at the same time. Needless to say, this economic inbreeding was not likely to benefit the financial health of the business, but it was in a sense inherent in the nature of the patronage that was being sought and bestowed.[31] Those who believed in the Wiener Werkstätte supported it in any way they could, and as long as their money held out, there was no real reason to worry about broadening the customer base. William Morris's ideal of simple crafts for the common people had been shattered by the high costs of producing handmade goods. Hoffmann had no such illusions. Hand in hand with his disdain for machine production went a tacit acknowledgment that Wiener Werkstätte products could and should be bought only by the well-to-do. "It is absolutely no longer possible to convert the masses," Hoffmann declared emphatically. "But then it is all the more our duty to make happy those few who turn to us."[32] Hoffmann, together with most of the avant-garde artists of his time and the upper middle class who supported them, constituted a self-chosen cultural elite that, by

36

37. Josef Hoffmann. Country
house designed for the Primavesi family, Winkelsdorf,
Czechoslovakia. 1913–14.
The combination of neoclassical columns with vernacular

features such as the thatched
roof and wooden siding is typical of Hoffmann's return to
traditional sources in the
years just prior to World
War I.

38. Josef Hoffmann. Bed-
room in the Primavesis' country house. 1913–14. Sketch by
Karl Bräuer.

birth and breeding, judged itself aesthetically superior to the
common man.

Essentially antidemocratic, the Wiener Werkstätte had no
desire to cater to plebeian tastes or budgets. "We neither can
nor will compete for the lowest prices," declared the work
program. "That is chiefly done at the worker's expense. We,
on the contrary, regard it as our highest duty to return him
to a position in which he can take pleasure in his labor and
lead a life in keeping with human dignity."[33] The word "workers" in this credo evokes the Morrisian socialist ethic, but in
practice, the Wiener Werkstätte was geared not to "workers"
in any Marxist sense, but to a rather elevated caste of artist/
craftsmen. One of the complaints that motivated the founding of the Werkstätte was that such products as silver were
sold merely by weight, without taking into account the value
of the designer's contribution. The Wiener Werkstätte was
devised principally to improve the working conditions of art-
ist/craftsmen by assuring them ample compensation and total
creative freedom. The Artists' Workshops may be seen as
an extension of this basic concept, providing artists with an
unlimited supply of materials with which to work and, ideally,
a guaranteed market for the results.[34] Morris's utopia

embraced all of society; the Wiener Werkstätte's only the
artistic community itself.

Neither Fritz Wärndorfer nor Otto Primavesi, the Wiener
Werkstätte's two principal financiers, ever viewed his investment in business terms. And both, in the course of their
involvement with the Werkstätte, were directly or indirectly
driven bankrupt by it. Primavesi's daughter recalled, "Our
only wish was to make it possible for the artists to do what
they wanted, it had nothing to do with business. When you
have a lot of money, you think you always will have money."[35]
Hoffmann readily admitted that the Werkstätte eschewed
business considerations to concentrate on "promoting good-
quality, beautiful work. We sought only the best materials."[36]
In keeping with this general attitude, the Wiener Werkstätte
did its best to accommodate the whims of its artist collaborators. Kokoschka remembered that, when only a student, he
requested and was given permission to use costly parchment
for a commemorative binding.[37] Although the artists were
ostensibly supposed to execute their own designs, Dagobert
Peche commandeered a little army of assistants and squan-
dered countless hours creating fanciful and costly extravagan-
zas. Even shoe buckles were finished in gilt. "Buy now, pay

later" was the basic philosophy, and the Wiener Werkstätte's cost overruns were legendary. The enterprise lived a hand-to-mouth existence, albeit on a lavish scale, constantly using its income to pay accumulated debts and then amassing more debts in order to continue its activities. The real goal, it came to seem, was to find the perfect *Milchkuh*, or milk cow—the one who would never run dry.

Things first came to a head, it appears, in 1906. Both Viktor Zuckerkandl and Alexander Brauner, for whom the Wiener Werkstätte had built a house on the Hohe Warte in 1905/06, felt they had been overcharged and were suing. Wärndorfer grimly wrote Hoffmann, "Karl W [Wittgenstein] has paid his bill … now we shall live, I think for another half year—and then it will be Stoclet's turn. May God help us further!"[38] Stoclet, apparently, did not take kindly to being used as the next *Milchkuh*; when his turn came, and he began to suspect that his money was not being employed for the intended purpose, he ceased making advance payments. The Wiener Werkstätte's growing financial troubles served to widen the gap between Hoffmann and Moser. In 1905 Moser had married Editha Mautner-Markhof, a former Kunstgewerbeschule student whose dining room he and Hoffmann had designed in 1904 (fig. 3). Moser was extremely sensitive about his wife's rather incredible wealth and took special pains to make sure that people understood that they kept their finances completely separate. Carl Moll felt that the marriage, in and of itself, alienated Moser from the rest of the group, but in any case, the final blow was struck when Wärndorfer, unbeknownst to Moser, approached Ditha for a loan of 100,000 kronen. Despite Moser's vehement objections, his wife did, in the end, give the Werkstätte 50,000 kronen, but Moser was through: he tendered his resignation in early 1907. "I will never give Fritz advice," he wrote Hoffmann. "But I am firmly convinced that, as it has been thus far, so it will always be—we will never manage to establish a healthy financial footing. How—I am not businessman enough to say. And much as I esteem you, I must nonetheless tell you that you, too, know nothing of business."[39]

Fritz Wärndorfer had long been looked upon with disapproval by his more conservative relatives. His brother August, a collector of Queen Anne silver, Japanese netsuke and Persian rugs, thought that the Wiener Werkstätte was sheer lunacy, and its financial woes seemed destined to prove him right.[40] In 1907 Wärndorfer sold off one of his family's cotton mills to obtain additional operating capital;[41] in 1909 the banks foreclosed,[42] but still, somehow, the Werkstätte went on. Finally, in the autumn of 1913, with an outstanding debt of 1.5 million kronen (well over a quarter of a million dollars at that time), everything came to a halt.[43] The Wärndorfer family made good, on behalf of its black sheep, the Wiener Werkstätte's entire debt, and the naughty boy was shipped off to America, at the time a not unusual punishment for such transgressions.[44] In 1914 the Wiener Werkstätte was liquidated and reorganized as a privately owned corporation (*Gesellschaft mit beschränkter Haftung*), with the largest number of shares held by the Primavesi family. In 1915 Otto Primavesi assumed the position of managing director. The Wiener Werkstätte had found another *Milchkuh*, and it was off and running.

39. Gustav Klimt. *Portrait of Mäda Primavesi*. Ca. 1912. Oil on canvas. 59″ × 43¼″. The sitter is the daughter of Eugenia and Otto Primavesi.

At first, Primavesi's administration seemed to be a success. As the heir to an immense fortune (his grandfather had founded the Primavesi Bank in Moravia, his father the Moravian sugar industry, and the family also controlled factories for the processing of jute and burlap[45]), Primavesi had impressive business and social contacts to offer the Wiener Werkstätte. He was instrumental in expanding the Werkstätte's participation in international trade fairs and also succeeded in attracting a more aristocratic clientele. The textile and fashion divisions, the most prosperous in the Wiener Werkstätte, appeared to be thriving in their new Kärntnerstrasse showrooms, and foreign branches were opening, so it seemed, at the rate of one or more a year. Whether Primavesi was merely throwing good money after bad or whether all these branches were actually at one point self-supporting is difficult to determine. At any rate, they began, one by one, to close. The New York branch nearly drove its founder, Josef Urban (an Austrian-born architect who had made good as chief set designer for the Metropolitan Opera), to bankruptcy. Urban, a cofounder of the Hagenbund, was close friends with many of the Werkstätte artists, and he sank almost his entire savings into the Fifth Avenue shop in an attempt to aid war-torn Austria.[46] The merchandise, which Urban insisted on buying outright rather than in a more conventional consignment arrangement, failed to sell, and in 1924 the shop closed its doors.[47] The Zürich branch, which

40

40. Josef Hoffmann. Bowl
designed for Eugenia (also
called Mäda) Primavesi. Ca.
1908. Silver. 2½″ high. Executed by the Wiener
Werkstätte.

for all intents and purposes ceased to operate in 1920, was officially removed from the trade registry in 1926.[48] The Berlin branch, opened in the disastrous year of 1929, hardly even got off the ground.

Philipp Häusler's attempt to reorganize the Wiener Werkstätte in the early 1920s had been well intentioned but unsuccessful. He found that Hoffmann's philosophy of allowing artists complete creative freedom had backfired into a system of collossal waste and ineptitude. Artists who were incapable of executing usable working drawings were nonetheless being paid for their efforts. Otto Primavesi, who really did believe himself to be the ultimate, soft-hearted *Milchkuh*, had given many of his destitute relatives jobs, both at the Wiener Werkstätte and in his own factories.[49] That these people were unqualified was a point that Häusler had a difficult time driving home, and in 1925 he was forced to leave. Primavesi, for his part, had no illusions about the impracticality of the Wiener Werkstätte's ideals, but he also recognized that there was no other way to run the workshops and still remain true to their original purpose. Considering the situation hopeless, he made a last-ditch attempt to salvage his other failing businesses and ended up completely alienating his wife, who wanted to save the Werkstätte at all costs.[50] In the midst of this atmosphere of economic and domestic turmoil, Primavesi suddenly took ill. Influenza developed into pneumonia, and in February 1926 he died; in April the Primavesi

bank failed. The Wiener Werkstätte went into receivership shortly thereafter but, miraculously, was granted yet one more reprieve: its creditors agreed to settle for 35 percent of their due, and the Werkstätte was back in business. Kuno Grohmann, a distant relative of Primavesi, now tried to rescue the operation by providing capital and business management.[51] Like Primavesi before him, Grohmann had primary obligations to his own factories and was unable to devote his full attention to the Wiener Werkstätte. He resigned his post in early 1930, and later that year his shares and those of the Primavesis were taken over by two new entrepreneurs, Alfred Hofmann, an Austrian, and Georges Oeri, a Swiss. By the end of 1931 it was clear that there was no hope: all the workers were dismissed, and the painful process of liquidating the inventory began. The coup de grâce was delivered by the auction house of Glückselig, which sold off the remaining merchandise in September 1932. The fashion department, which in 1931 had been forced to move in with the textile division, lingered on until November, as it was still possible to sell some of its products at full price.

There are many reasons that can and have been cited for the Wiener Werkstätte's decline: the refusal to fully industrialize, the inability to cater to a broader public, and the squandering of resources in the name of art. While it is clear from the Wärndorfer experience that the Werkstätte was never financially stable, the primary blame for its demise still must be placed on the changes wrought by World War I. After all, if the Werkstätte had, so to speak, been bankrupt from the start, it would never have survived the nearly thirty years that it did. As long as there were people to buy its products and backers to provide funding, the enterprise could, theoretically, have gone on indefinitely. If the conditions that had prevailed prior to the war had continued, it might have. Given a healthier financial climate, it might yet have been rescued. Certain of its activities—the expansion of the retail market, the undeniable success of the fashion and textile divisions—suggest as much. The Werkstätte might even have seen the light and been pursuaded to design for industry—if Austria had had any industry to speak of. But most of the Austrian empire's factories had been built in the outlying provinces of Moravia and Bohemia, and near Budapest, areas that now belonged to the newly formed nations of Czechoslovakia and Hungary. Primavesi, whose factories were located in Moravia, found himself constantly at odds with Czech nationals, who loathed the German-speaking minority that had once ruled them. Further complicating matters were the unfavorable currency exchange regulations now governing territories that had previously been one nation.[52] The immediate postwar period saw inflation on a magnitude that can hardly be imagined. (The artist Alfred Kubin recalled in his autobiography that he and his wife, at the time, owned some houses in Germany and considered themselves secure. However, they sold the buildings and with the proceeds, "by acting fast," were just able to buy a new stove.)[53] Inflation made most paper investments worthless and wiped out the savings of many middle-class families. Currency stabilization in the mid-1920s brought some semblance of normalcy, but the American stock market crash of 1929 triggered a depression that gradually spread to all parts of Europe.

It is easy, in retrospect, to say that the dissolution of the Austrian empire was inevitable, but regardless of the ingrained pessimism that is native to Vienna, very few people in 1914 (including the iconoclastic Adolf Loos),[54] expected the war to be lost or the monarchy to collapse. From this perspective, the circumstances of the postwar era can only be viewed as extraordinary: not a fitting culmination to all that came before, but a drastic turn of events that cut off the course of development and denied prewar innovations their natural denouement. What would all those eager Kunstgewerbeschule graduates have achieved had not the entire economic base of their future livelihoods been rent asunder? War, sickness, and the privations resulting from war wiped out many of the most promising talents: Klimt, Lendecke, Moser, and Schiele died in 1918; Dagobert Peche, who had replaced Moser in spirit at the Wiener Werkstätte, died in 1923; Julius Zimpel, Peche's successor, died in 1925. Many of those who were left alive felt compelled to abandon Austria for more stable and prosperous nations. Already in 1907, Czeschka had left his post at the Kunstgewerbeschule to teach in Hamburg, together with Richard Luksch. Kokoschka remained in Dresden after the war, and only returned briefly to Vienna. Eduard Wimmer, the founder of the Werkstätte's fashion department, went to America in 1922; the ceramicist Vally Wieselthier followed in 1929.

Instead of gliding gracefully into the twentieth century, Austria lost not only her industrialized former provinces, but most of the talents who had contributed to the *fin-de-siècle* renaissance.

In the postwar climate, the efforts of the Wiener Werkstätte looked silly, and Loos's criticisms of Hoffmann, once so potent, sounded shrill. The art historian Hans Tietze noted of the 1920 Kunstschau that "in the light of the deadly earnest of the present time, and of that restriction to barest essentials which is acknowledged by all and sundry as being unavoidable, the exhibition of a thousand amiable trifles strikes one as untimely, even eerie."[55] The Werkstätte's contributions to the Paris Art Deco exhibition of 1925 were not well received, and Loos took the opportunity to launch what he must have considered a final assault on a movement he had long considered impractical and amoral. Other attacks and counterattacks followed, libel suits were lodged, but the ultimate effect was that of beating a dead (or dying) horse. If the socialists, who were now assuming a more dominant role in Austria, perceived a certain decadence in the Wiener Werkstätte's efforts to carry on, it was decadence of a most benign, even pathetic, variety.

The social structure that had sustained the Wiener Werkstätte was crumbling. There were no more Stoclets to commission lavish palaces, no more Primavesis to pour capital into an economically unviable venture merely because they believed in its principles. There was, quite simply, no more capital. The Werkstätte had never really been designed to be self-supporting. As an artist-run business enterprise it had, from its inception, embodied certain contradictions that were destined to be self-defeating. The artists of the Werkstätte found the notion of a neutral, capitalistically oriented cultural intermediary—such as had taken over the purveyance of art in Germany and France—morally repugnant. It is ironic that Egon Schiele, shortly before he died, was plotting a grand new cutural enterprise, which he called a Kunsthalle, incorporating many of the old ideals and problems of the Secession and the Wiener Werkstätte. Supported through sales exhibitions and the translation of foreign poetry, the Kunsthalle would use its proceeds to aid needy young artists and establish a museum of modern art; it was to be "its own dealer and publisher—that is the most important thing."[56] Austrian artists harbored a pervasive fear of relinquishing the control they had long maintained over the distribution of their work, for they feared that if business considerations were to enter this realm, all aesthetic ideals would of necessity be sacrificed. To achieve such a utopian paradigm as that put forth by the Kunsthalle, or the Wiener Werkstätte, or the Secession in its early days, required a conspiracy of artists and patrons to override normal economic conditions in pursuit of an ideal creative environment. One may call it an unrealistic dream, but it must be said that while the dream lasted, it generated some of the most compellingly exquisite objects of the twentieth century. Moser, in his parting from the Wiener Werkstätte, had noted, "Nobody can live this way—except in terms of creating art for the benefit of posterity."[57] In the end, this is exactly what the Werkstätte produced: a legacy that included many near perfect achievements, of which we, today, are the beneficiaries.

1

1. Carl Moll. *Breakfast.* Ca.
1903. Oil on canvas. Signed,
lower left. 60½″ × 60½″. The
setting of the painting is probably a room in one of the villas on
the Hohe Warte designed by
Josef Hoffmann. The coffee
service in the foreground is by
Jutta Sika (compare with Fig.
104).

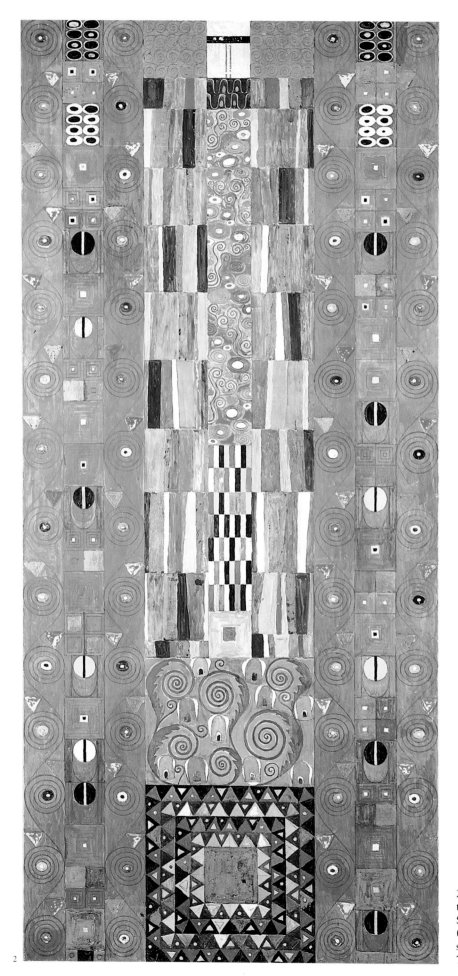

2. Gustav Klimt. Design for the back wall of the Palais Stoclet dining room. Ca. 1905–09. Tempera, watercolor, gold, silver and pencil on paper. 77½″ × 35⅞″.

3

3. Gustav Klimt. *Fulfillment
(Embrace)*. Ca.1905–09. Tempera, watercolor, gold, silver
and pencil on paper.
76⅜″ × 47⅝″. Design for the
main wall of the Palais Stoclet
dining room.

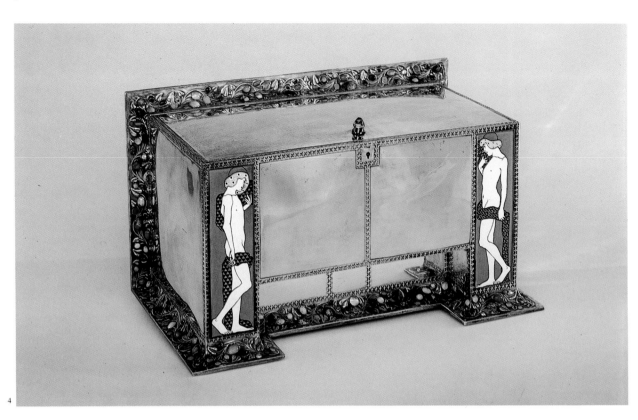

4

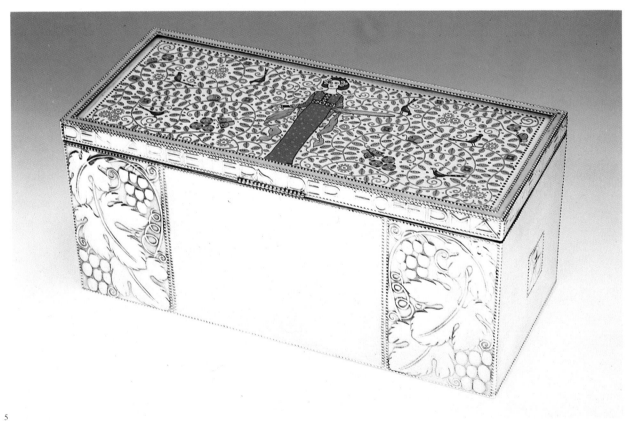

5

4. Koloman Moser. Decorative box. 1906. Silver with semi-precious stones and enamel insets. 9½" high. Executed by Adolf Erbrich and Karl Ponocny for the Wiener Werkstätte.

5. Josef Hoffmann. Decorative box. 1910. Silver, with painted parchment cover inset by Carl Krenek. 10½" long. Executed by the Wiener Werkstätte as a tribute to the workers of the Falkenstein company.

6

6. Gustav Klimt. *Portrait of
Eugenia (Mäda) Primavesi*. Ca.
1913–14. Oil on canvas. Signed,
lower right. 55⅛″ × 33⅛″.
Eugenia Primavesi was the wife
of Otto Primavesi, the Wiener
Werkstätte's last major backer.

7. Josef Diveky (attr.). Cabaret
Fledermaus, Vienna; barroom
designed by the Wiener Werkstätte and decorated with tiles
produced by the Wiener Keramik. Ca. 1907–08. Color lithograph postcard (No. 74).
5½" × 3½". Published by the
Wiener Werkstätte.

8

8. Berthold Löffler. *Kunst-schau Wien, 1908.* Color lithograph poster. 27″ × 37¾″. Printed by Albert Berger.

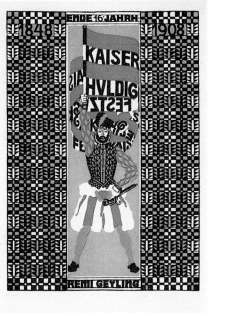

9

10

9. Remigus Geyling. *Parade in Honor of the Emperor, Late 16th Century.* 1908. Color lithograph postcard (No. 177). 5½″ × 3½″. Published by the Wiener Werkstätte.

10. Remigus Geyling. *Military Procession, Late 16th Century.* 1908. Color lithograph postcard (No. 167). 5½″ × 3½″. Published by the Wiener Werkstätte.

11. Otto Wagner. Competition
design for the Postsparkasse
(Postal Savings Bank). 1903.
Watercolor, pen and ink and
pencil with white highlighting.
Inscribed, upper left.
33⅝″ × 16⅜″.

11

ARCHITECTURE AND THE GRAND IDEAL

Architecture was the mother art form of the *Gesamtkunstwerk* in its practical incarnation, just as opera was the mother of the *Gesamtkunstwerk* in its theatrical incarnation. The Wiener Werkstätte hoped to create complete environments by uniting, under the direction of an architect, an ensemble of players composed of everything from paperhangers to painters to cabinetmakers.

At first, when Hoffmann and Moser were the main designers, it proved relatively simple to blend the various subordinate elements harmoniously. During this formative period, in which the *Gesamtkunstwerk* achieved its most effective realization, three principal architectural styles exerted, in succession, a dominant influence. Austria's adaptation of Art Nouveau conditioned the early years of the Hoffmann/Moser collaboration, which began around the turn of the century, shortly after the founding of the Secession. At the height of the collaboration, reached around 1904, the style became considerably more severe, emphasizing simplicity and structural unity. Subsequently, the two men went their separate ways, and Hoffmann returned to the historical and vernacular models that had interested him from his student years.

THE BEGINNINGS

Josef Maria Olbrich was probably the most important Viennese representative of the first, or Art Nouveau, phase of *fin-de-siècle* architecture, and his best-known building in Austria, the Secession, was one of the most significant examples of the style (fig. 43). His approach was not unlike that of his mentor, Otto Wagner, for whom he worked, and it is likely that the two men exerted a mutual influence on one another. From Wagner came the essentially classical base form that characterized much Viennese Art Nouveau, and from the younger man came the love of *Jugendstil* floral ornament. In the case of Wagner's designs for the Stadtbahn (intracity railroad) stations, it is sometimes hard to parcel out responsibility for the different elements, but it has been suggested that the ornate wrought-iron decor was in fact Olbrich's contribution[1] (fig. 41). The domed, cathedrallike structure of Olbrich's Secession building, on the other hand, owes a clear debt to Wagner's classicism (Wagner would devise a similar scheme for the Steinhof church [fig. 42]) and was also especially appropriate to a building that the architect

41

41. Otto Wagner. Sketch for the Vienna *Stadtbahn* (intracity railroad), Karlsplatz station (detail). 1894-99. Watercolor, pen and ink, pencil and gold, with white highlighting. Inscribed, upper right. 25⅝" × 18⅛".

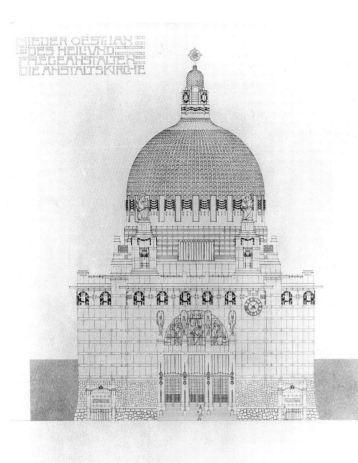

42. Otto Wagner. Sketch for
the Steinhof church, Vienna;
main façade. 1904. Pen and
ink and pencil. Inscribed,
upper left and lower right.
26¾" × 19¼".

43. Josef Maria Olbrich.
Poster for the second and
third Secession exhibitions.
1898-99. Color lithograph.
33½" × 19⅞". Printed by
Albert Berger.

considered a temple of art. Critics have complained that the
decorative and classical elements are clumsily handled in the
Secession building, and indeed all Olbrich's work could be
accused of a certain sloppiness—sensational effects superimposed on ungainly, hastily conceived structures. Nonetheless,
there was much to admire in this young dynamo. "He was,
in his own way, a volcano, a fire-breather," Wagner later
wrote. "He did not limit himself to architecture, he worked
with arts and crafts, designed furniture, sketched carpets,
modelled vases. He was inexhaustible in his ideas, comprehensive in his undertakings."[2] Watercolorist, sculptor and
even musician as well as designer, Olbrich was the marvel of
his friends and colleagues, as energetic at play as at work. In
his varied endeavors, and his concern with coordinating the
interior together with the exterior of a building, he must be
considered a formative influence on the slightly younger artists of the Wiener Werkstätte.

   By 1898, when the Secession building opened, Olbrich
had left Wagner's office and opened his own studio. As a

rising young talent, he had a promising future to look forward to in Vienna, but in 1899, after failing to land a post at
the Kunstgewerbeschule despite Wagner's recommendation,
he decided to take a job at the Mathildenhöhe artists' colony
near Darmstadt. Olbrich's departure for Germany left the
way open for his younger colleague, Josef Hoffmann, who
received the Kunstgewerbeschule appointment instead of
him. Why this post was granted to a younger man who had
yet to execute his first entire building is perhaps explained by
the controversy surrounding the Secession edifice. Olbrich
was perceived as a radical, and so he was passed over in favor
of a less accomplished but seemingly "safer" choice who also
happened to be a favorite of Wagner's. Up until this time,
Hoffmann had existed largely in Olbrich's shadow. Born in
1870, he was the youngest of the three most influential members of the *Siebener Klub*. Just as he admired Koloman
Moser, whose experiences as an illustrator earning money in
the "real" world made him seem glamorously adult, so, too,
he must have been dazzled by the light of Olbrich's bright

star. After the *Siebener Klub* merged into the Secession, it was Olbrich who received the commission for the new building and Moser who designed the exterior ornamentation for the façade (fig. 45), while Hoffmann was assigned the display rooms for the organization's publication, *Ver Sacrum*. Hoffmann's Secession interiors, however, began to win him notice in his own right, and one of the last projects that he executed in tandem with Olbrich—a number of the Austrian rooms at the 1900 Paris World's Fair—was instrumental in establishing his reputation. The success of the Austrian avant-garde when, for the first time, it presented its innovations to an international audience was acknowledged by the emperor himself, who in 1901 bestowed upon Hoffmann the Cross of the Knight of the Order of Franz Josef.

During the years just prior to the turn of the century, Hoffmann had been occupied with absorbing and reconciling a number of formative influences. Like Olbrich and his future nemesis Adolf Loos, he had been born in that part of the empire that is now Czechoslovakia, and in fact he attended both the same *Gymnasium* and technical school as Loos. Early exposure to this relatively industrialized area of Austro-Hungary, as well as to the indigenous peasant architecture that dotted the countryside, helped shape the creative visions of all three architects. At the Vienna Academy of Fine Art, Hoffmann came under the tutelage of Otto Wagner, who infected him with a lifelong respect for the principles of classical architecture. He had ample opportunity to study such architecture in the original after receiving the prestigious Rome prize for his final project in 1895. Travel in Italy confirmed his feeling that "what mattered above all was the proportion, and that even the most accurate application of the individual forms of architecture meant nothing at all."[3] In addition to classical models, he was also drawn to humble native dwellings, discovering that "the simple yet specially characteristic Italian way of building . . . had more to say to our effort to arrive at form by doing justice to purpose and material."[4] Thus Hoffmann strove to understand and assimilate the underlying principles of classical and vernacular architecture rather than merely imitating the superficial forms. On his return to Vienna, these ideas began to merge with new foreign influences, such as Art Nouveau curves and British ideals of craftsmanship, to condition the young architect's earliest interiors (fig. 46). Art Nouveau became the "style"— the source of surface ornament—while classical and vernacular principles of construction, filtered through an arts and crafts sieve, became the underlying inspiration. Insofar as Art Nouveau was never central to this conception, it remained only to be discarded before Hoffmann could head out on the road to establishing his own aesthetic.

The decisive moment came with a commission to build a group of villas on the Hohe Warte, a hill in one of Vienna's more bucolic outlying districts. Hoffmann's first assignment involving the construction of complete buildings, it was among the opportunities that Olbrich had abandoned when he left for Germany. The ideal venue for the *Gesamtkunstwerk*, Olbrich and his Secessionist colleagues agreed, would be an entire city.[5] However, lacking any chance of realizing such a dream, four of the artists—Carl Moll, Moser, Hugo Henneberg, and Friedrich Spitzer—decided to commission a

44

45

44. Josef Maria Olbrich. Candlestick, plate and cutlery. Ca. 1900–1902. Silver plate.

45. Koloman Moser. Wall decoration for the exterior of the Secession building, Vienna. 1898.

residential colony. When Olbrich, the obvious architect of choice, proved too busy with his new duties in Darmstadt to devote proper attention to the project, Moll fired him and the job went to Hoffmann. The four houses, built between 1900 and 1902, show a continuing refinement of geometric forms, coupled with a more conscious attempt to come to terms with the British crafts idiom (fig. 48). The sinuous curves that had characterized Hoffmann's previous interiors, as well as some of the more fanciful designs he had worked out on paper for never-executed projects, were honed down under the pressures of so ambitious an undertaking. Possibly Moser also influenced his turn to a more linear aesthetic. It has been suggested that Moser collaborated on the interiors of his own house[6] (fig. 47), and this theory is borne out by the fact that some of these interiors were illustrated in *Deutsche Kunst und Dekoration* as Moser's work.[7] At any rate, the decorative scheme of the Hohe Warte houses represents a new

46. Josef Hoffmann. "Gray
Room," designed for the
fourth Secession exhibition.
1899.

47. Koloman Moser.
Entrance hall in his own
home. Ca. 1905.

48. Carl Moll. *Garden Ter-
race of the Artist's Home on
the Hohe Warte*. 1903. Oil on
canvas. Signed, lower right.
39⅜" × 39⅜".

direction for Hoffmann, with cheerful colors (carried through
in painted furniture and ceramic tile insets) set off against
white stucco walls. The half-timbering used on the exteriors
of the houses, on the other hand, is a rather less congenial
leftover from the British mode. While the revival of medieval
tradition had been important to the British, it was to prove
irrelevant for the Austrians, whose roots were more classical
and whose climate demanded different practical solutions.
Other British antecedents may be found in the idea of the
"artist's cottage" and the unifying central hall. However, the
Hohe Warte villas can hardly be called cottages, and they
reached not back to a quaint rural past, but forward to a new
conception of unified spatial design and urbane elegance.
Similarly, the concept of the hall and staircase was adapted,
especially in the Spitzer and Henneberg houses, to mediate
between the volumes of the various stories in an entirely original manner.

THE PURIST PHASE

With the Hohe Warte villas, Hoffmann had begun the
process of winnowing out those aspects of the British crafts
model that were to be of lasting significance to him. Possibly
his trip to England in 1902 further helped him to separate
the superficial, stylistically oriented aspects of the movement
from the underlying principles—such as functionalism and
craftsmanship—that he considered increasingly important.
Mackintosh's formulation of a "styleless style"—i.e., one that
had no specific references to the past—exerted a powerful
influence in the wake of the Secession's 1900 exhibition of
European design, but it must be remembered that it was just
in these two points—functionalism and craftsmanship—that
Mackintosh was weakest. The classic Mackintosh chair is
beautiful but uncomfortable (fig. 19), and his work is often
criticized for its shoddy construction.[8] If the Mackintosh aes-

thetic, characterized by black furniture set off against white walls, was nonetheless seductive, credit for the isolation and emphasis of geometric motifs must also be given to Moser. Moser introduced a new two-dimensional graphic sensibility, which Hoffmann, a master of spatial design, carried to its ultimate three-dimensional conclusion. Their most important collaborative project, and the first major commission undertaken by the Wiener Werkstätte, was the Purkersdorf Sanatorium.

The Purkersdorf Sanatorium (figs. 49–55), a spa for the treatment of nervous disorders, was one of those peculiar institutions favored by the European upper classes: part resort and part hospital. This duality of function was reflected very clearly in the overall design—the severe, practical treatment rooms in sharp opposition to the sumptuous public areas. The purpose of each particular area was taken into consideration in the design of every detail, so that, for exam-

ple, the chairs in the music room were intentionally more commodious than those in the hall, where people were not expected to linger. The sanatorium, built between 1904 and 1905, was the first project in which the Wiener Werkstätte could attempt a realization of a *Gesamtkunstwerk* on a grand scale. Everything but the kitchen utensils was designed and, with the exception of the textiles, produced by the Werkstätte. The building itself represents a stripped-down version of Wagner's classicism, in which the only ornamentation on the flat, and flat-roofed, white façade is provided by Richard Luksch's reliefs near the entrance (fig. 49) and by the ceramic tile insets, whose shape, in turn, is echoed by the neat, square windows. This motif is carried through in the central hall to the cubic chairs, which have been variously attributed to both Hoffmann and Moser[9] (fig. 51). The hall itself continues Hoffmann's experiments from the later Hohe Warte houses in its play of spatial volumes and levels (fig. 50).

Meanwhile, all superficial allusions to the British style have disappeared or been submerged in the architect's native classicism. Perhaps the most innovative aspect of the entire design was Hoffmann's decision to leave the ferro-concrete interior supports exposed (fig. 54), a solution that heretofore had been used almost exclusively for so-called engineer's structures, such as exhibition pavilions or train stations.

In the austerity of its geometric solutions—which were unrelentingly evoked throughout the interior and exterior spaces and surfaces—the Purkersdorf Sanatorium may be considered the purest project of the purist phase of Austrian architecture. Any number of factors called forth an increasing richness of decoration in the next years. For one thing, not every commission could be a hospital, and the wealthy clients of the Wiener Werkstätte wanted homes that reflected their status. For another, the reliance on painted walls and furniture impaired the ability of the materials to speak for themselves, as was encouraged by both the crafts ethic and Hoffmann's love of luxurious detailing, rare woods and colored marble. Finally, new collaborators such as Carl Otto Czeschka, Berthold Löffler and Michael Powolny (the latter two cofounders of the Wiener Keramik) introduced a fresh ornamentalism to the Werkstätte's formal devices. This new tendency may be seen in the Hochreith hunting lodge, decorated for Karl Wittgenstein in 1906 (fig. 57), and found its ultimate expression in the Wiener Werkstätte's ultimate commission, the Palais Stoclet on the Avenue de Tervueren in Brussels (frontispiece, figs. 58 and 59).

Adolf Stoclet, a Belgian industrialist, met Hoffmann in 1902 under the most casual of circumstances. Stoclet and his wife, on a visit to Vienna, took a walk along the Hohe Warte and were caught snooping about in Moll's backyard. When Stoclet expressed his admiration for the house, Moll offered to introduce him to the architect, and did so that very day. It was Stoclet's original intention to commission a similar villa on the Hohe Warte, but his father's sudden death in 1904 sent him back to Brussels a millionaire, and a Belgian palace on a much more lavish scale was planned instead. From the start, it was apparent that the Palais Stoclet was to be a *tour de force*: all the stops were to be pulled out, no expense was to be spared. What the three-story, forty-odd-room house ended up costing will remain forever a secret, though it is known that the materials for Klimt's dining room frieze alone came to 100,000 kronen (pls. 2 and 3, fig. 58). During the protracted period of construction, from approximately 1905 to 1911, plans were worked and reworked without any regard for the impact such changes might have on the ill-defined budget. Throughout the house only the best, most costly materials were used: real gold and jewels adorned the figures in Klimt's frieze; rare, colored marble was carefully matched and affixed both to the exterior and to many of the interior rooms; the ultimate in craftsmanship, from marquetry to mosaic work, was applied to the decorative detailing. Not only did the Wiener Werkstätte supervise every detail, including a special silver service, but it also employed an army of outside artists and artisans on the project. Leopold Forstner, a Kunstgewerbeschule graduate who had recently opened his own mosaic studio, executed Klimt's frieze, the Wiener Keramik produced tiles, and Ludwig Heinrich Jung-

49

50

49. Josef Hoffmann. Purkers-dorf Sanatorium, Vienna; view of the main entrance, with wall reliefs by Richard Luksch. 1904.

50. Josef Hoffmann and Koloman Moser. Purkersdorf Sanatorium; view of the main hall, facing the entrance. 1904.

51

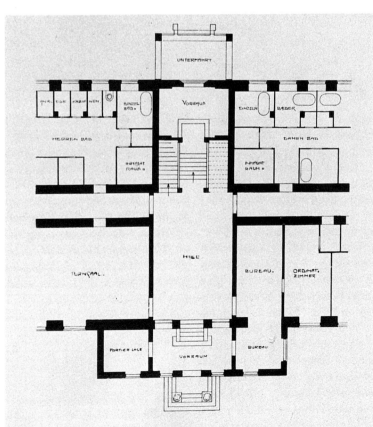

52

51. Josef Hoffmann and Koloman Moser. Purkersdorf Sanatorium; seating arrangement, main hall. 1904.

52. Josef Hoffmann. Purkersdorf Sanatorium; plan of the entrance and main hall. 1904.

53. Josef Hoffmann. Chair designed for the dining hall of the Purkersdorf Sanatorium. 1904. Polished beechwood. 38¾″ high. Executed by Jacob & Josef Kohn.

53

nickel designed a frieze for the children's room. In addition to this, there were the designs that were commissioned and then rejected, such as Kokoschka's needlework adaptation of his illustrated book, *Die träumenden Knaben* (The Dreaming Boys) (fig. 190), or Schiele's proposal for a stained-glass window (fig. 192).

The flat roof and linear geometry of the Stoclet house were a repetition of elements already evident in the Purkersdorf project, though the sumptuousness of the palace's decorative scheme, by its very nature, superceded the tectonic originality of the sanatorium by concealing rather than exploiting the means of construction. The motif of the hall here encountered its most original presentation to date; it became a two-story atrium, surrounded by a gallery on the upper level and linking the floors vertically and horizontally. The use of the hall and other superficial decorative details of the Stoclet project are reminiscent of Mackintosh's designs for a *Haus eines Kunstfreundes* (House for an Art Lover), which had been published in a portfolio called *Meister der Innenkunst* (Masters of Interior Decoration) in 1902.[10] However, whereas Mackintosh still incorporates geometric motifs as surface ornament, in Hoffmann's design the richness of the

marble cladding allows the walls to function as decoration without actually being decorated, and brings the real art— such as the Klimt frieze or Stoclet's own collection of antiquities and modern art—to the fore. While Mackintosh remains fussy and artsy-craftsy, Hoffmann's conception has been purified by the classical influence and by the imperative of the *Gesamtkunstwerk*.

The entire Palais Stoclet was conceived as a monumental sculpture, with two- and three-dimensional forms so intimately wedded that, as in the "poor rich man's" house caricatured by Loos, there was not a detail that could be added, removed or changed without altering the whole. It was, in Loos's words, "complete"—a perfect *Gesamtkunstwerk* from the sculptures in the garden to the teaspoons in the pantry. Though surprisingly little publicized at the time, the Stoclet mansion was to become one of Hoffmann's most influential works, admired by such later designers as Le Corbusier, Gerrit Rietveld, and Mies van der Rohe. The project represented a phase in Hoffmann's development in which the various elements—classicism and severity, simplicity and opulence— were in total harmony. As it turned out, this was a short-lived phase, and indeed the Stoclet house itself could never have been realized were it not for the unusual circumstances of the commission. The latent trend of Hoffmann's work, already hinted at in the Stoclet building, was conservative, for in coming to terms with his classical background, he was already beginning to toe the fine line between tradition and historicism.

TRADITIONALISM

Hoffmann's original credo—that one must incorporate the precepts but not the specific forms of the past—already showed signs of being compromised in his pavilion for the 1908 Kunstschau (fig. 68). An international exhibition held in Rome in 1911, however, provided the excuse for a complete exploitation of a renewed traditionalism. The allusion to antiquity implied by the setting begged to be consciously expressed in Hoffmann's exhibition hall, and classical motifs seemed particularly appropriate to the political significance of such an exposition. A similar solution was used, quite effectively and to great acclaim, for the Austrian pavilion at the mammoth Werkbund exhibition in Cologne in 1914 (fig. 61). Although Hoffmann protested that his new work was not historicist in the usual, oft-maligned sense, since he always took into account the demands of each particular situation, there is no escaping the fact that it represented a departure from his more purely original work of the early 1900s.

The return to a somewhat modernized variant of historicism had already emerged in the work of Olbrich and Behrens in Germany, and after 1906 it began sweeping all of Europe. In Austria there was a movement away from the alien and foreign, and toward everything that represented national values.[11] In keeping with this trend, the Biedermeier style came in for renewed scrutiny, as did the rural and indigenous styles of the provinces. This proclivity was strengthened by the association between avant-garde painting and folk art, put forth in the *Blaue Reiter Almanac* (published in

54

54. Josef Hoffmann. Purkersdorf Sanatorium; dining hall.
1904.

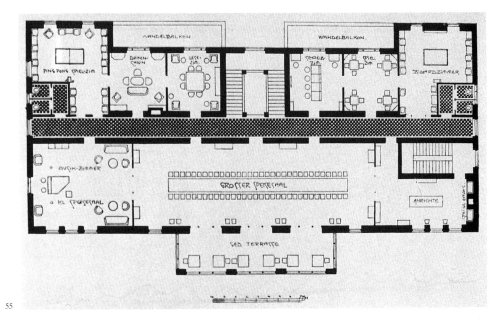

55

55. Josef Hoffmann. Purkersdorf Sanatorium; plan of the
dining hall and public rooms.
1904.

Munich in 1912). But in architecture the trend was reactionary rather than progressive—a retreat inward, away from a pan-European aesthetic. Hoffmann and the Wiener Werkstätte adapted very organically to this shift in direction. The architect had never entirely abandoned his interest in vernacular architecture, nor had he ever truly embraced urban values. Similarly, the crafts orientation of the Wiener Werkstätte facilitated the rejection of an industrialized lifestyle and provided a natural breeding ground for folk forms.

Perhaps one of the most complete expressions of this new, folkish[12] direction was the house that Hoffmann built for the Wiener Werkstätte's second great backer, Otto Primavesi, in Winkelsdorf (now in Czechoslovakia) between 1913 and 1914 (figs. 37 and 38). Together, the sculptor Anton Hanak, Mrs. Primavesi and Hoffmann cooked up the idea of a house that would reflect, both in style and in the almost exclusive use of local materials, regional peasant architecture.[13] This was a *Gesamtkunstwerk* in a new key—a full-fledged log house, complete with thatched roof, cheerful, painted "peasant" furniture and carvings, hand-embroidered bed linens, and even casually elegant silk robes that the Primavesis' frequent houseguests were supposed to wear to dinner. Every detail was designed by the Wiener Werkstätte to evoke a bucolic utopia, "not the way it really was, but the way we dreamed it should be," Mrs. Primavesi's daughter remembered.[14] She

sented symbolically by an American industrialist.[15] The friction that existed between Austria's idealized past and its imagined future was the impetus behind many of the *fin-de-siècle* innovations, which seemed so radical but actually had a solid understructure of conservatism.

ADOLF LOOS

The enmity that existed between Loos and Hoffmann is certainly well documented in Loos's many polemics against the Wiener Werkstätte, but it remains difficult to pinpoint, especially as Hoffmann's work went through numerous phases rather than representing a single unchanging stance. In truth the two men had much in common. They were both loyal to the classical traditions of Wagner, and they both incorporated historical elements in their work (while remaining united in their opposition to the Ringstrasse variant of historicism). Although Loos (like everyone else) paid lip service to an "art of the people," he (again like everyone else) owed his livelihood to the patronage of wealthy clients. Furthermore, despite his crusades against ornament, his work was not totally unornamented, and like Hoffmann he had a taste for expensive veneers and admired exquisite craftsmanship. The difference between the two men lay in the balance

56

also recalled, however, that her own room, with its busy blue-patterned wallpaper, could be oppressive, and that she sometimes felt compelled to retreat to the woodshed.

The dream of a different life-style—more true to an idealized peasant heritage, more true to a past that was by definition superior to the present—went hand in hand with an innate Austrian feeling of dissatisfaction that was, paradoxically, also a spur toward progressive innovation. Thus Hoffmann could reject historicism while at the same time permitting it to resurface in his own work, and his enemy, Adolf Loos, could simultaneously revile Austria for being backward and criticize Hoffmann for his antihistoricist stance. Both these men were attempting to marshal the same conflicting impulses: tradition and innovation, conservatism and progress, the countryside and the city, craftsmanship and industrialization, decoration and functionalism. Austria lived in fear and awe of the future, as satirized in Alfred Kubin's surrealistic novel, *Die andere Seite* (The Other Side), in which a dream kingdom, constituted as "a place of asylum for those who are disgusted with modern culture," is systematically destroyed by contact with the real world, as repre-

that each tried to strike between the various elements of style and structure, and, increasingly, in the inconsistencies which Loos delighted in finding in Hoffmann's approach.

Initially, it almost appeared that Hoffmann and Loos might have been friends. Although Loos never joined the Secession, he published a not unfavorable article on Hoffmann, as well as "Potemkin's Town," in *Ver Sacrum*. However, when he offered to design a room for the Secession, Hoffmann turned him down, and it may be that the rivalry stemmed from that moment. As Hoffmann became more successful, Loos, the more difficult and challenging architect, began to accuse him of stealing his ideas—and even his tailor.[16] The small-town environment of Vienna, in which petty jealousies frequently developed into full-scale enmities, did the rest. From the start, the author of "Potemkin's Town" had cautioned against taking too dogmatic a stand against historicism. "For me tradition is everything," Loos wrote, "the free activity of the imagination only secondary."[17] Loos believed in the industrial future that he had glimpsed on his travels in America, because he believed that it was here that the future linked up with the past. He felt that the pure

57

56. Carl Otto Czeschka.
Laquerwork panels designed
for the vestibule of the Hochreith hunting lodge. 1906.

57. Josef Hoffmann. Hoch-
reith hunting lodge, Lower
Austria; vestibule with decorative panels by Carl Otto
Czeschka, Josef Hoffmann,
Richard Luksch (ceramics)
and Koloman Moser (attr.,
glass). 1906.

58

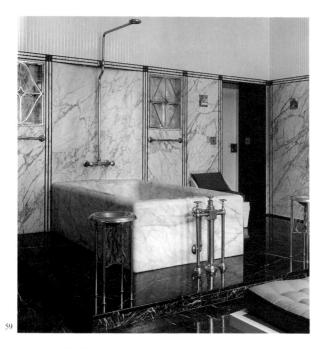

59

58. Josef Hoffmann. Palais
Stoclet, Brussels; dining room
with frieze designed by Gustav
Klimt and executed by Leopold Forstner. 1905–11.

59. Josef Hoffmann. Palais
Stoclet; bathroom. 1905–11.

machine (and in this sense a plow or a saddle is as much a machine as a turbine or a locomotive) is also the purest example of design because its form and its function are synonymous. Although Hoffmann professed similar beliefs, his fascination with newness—innovation for its own sake—implicitly violated the concept of functionalism, which is ageless. What Loos called the "free activity of the imagination" (and Hoffmann's strong point was undoubtedly his great inventive facility) was directly opposed to functionalism in its strictest form. Hoffmann's return to tradition in some respects brought him nearer to Loos's viewpoint, and Loos grudgingly admitted that, "insofar as construction is concerned [he] has gotten closer to my method." However, Loos remained convinced that there was more style than substance to his rival's work, and this criticism was at least partly justified by Hoffmann's increasing interest in surface decoration. Hoffmann, groused Loos, "still believes today that he can beautify his furniture with remarkable staining, patterning and superimposed ornamentation. Nevertheless, the modern man regards an untattooed surface as more beautiful than a tattooed one, even if the tattooing were to be done by Michelangelo himself."[18] In this, he invoked what he considered a fundamental distinction between art and utilitarian objects, as put forth by his friend Karl Kraus in his dictum about the chamberpot and the urn: "Loos and I, " wrote Kraus, "have done nothing further but to demonstrate that there is a difference between an urn and a chamberpot, and that therein lies the principal realm of culture. The others ... may be divided between those who use the urn as a chamberpot and those who use the chamberpot as an urn."[19] The logical corollary of the *Gesamtkunstwerk* premise—the leveling of art and craft—was to grant neither one its proper place.

Loos's buildings were less pleasing to the Viennese public than those of Hoffmann and the Wiener Werkstätte, and his career lacked the official stamp of approval that was given to Hoffmann in so many small but significant ways. Many of Loos's commissions consisted of private structures: residential buildings in Vienna's outlying districts, or commercial interiors, such as the Ebenstein and Knize tailoring establishments, or the minuscule, mirrored "American Bar." Out of sight, as they say, is out of mind, and such commissions did not create nearly the furor that did Loos's most highly visible building on the Michaelerplatz, opposite the north entrance to the Hofburg (the imperial residence). Loos built the apartment building-cum-storefront for the firm of Goldman and Salatsch—the tailors who dressed both him and Hoffmann in the fashionable "English" manner—between 1909 and 1911. Just as Hoffmann, in his Purkersdorf Sanatorium, had made a visual distinction between the treatment rooms and the entertainment areas, so Loos's façade reflected the division between the shop on the first floors and the apartment units in the upper stories. Whereas the lower section of the building was quite sumptuous (the use of marble cladding and classical columns suggests aspects of Hoffmann's work of this period), the upper portion was painfully austere. "No eyebrows!" gasped the emperor when he saw the unadorned window frames for the first time, and thereafter he refused to use the north gate. Loos cast himself as a loner, not only in his conscious rejection of ornament, but in his secondary career as a polemicist who, like his friend Kraus, deliberately set out to attack established Austrian values. He became the leader of a new band of isolated artists, including Oskar Kokoschka and Arnold Schoenberg, whose intensity of expression depended on a uniqueness that rendered unobtainable the social esteem accorded the more communally oriented Wiener Werkstätte.

EXHIBITION WORK

The communality of the Secession and later the Wiener Werkstätte was ideally reflected in the exhibitions mounted by these organizations. The exhibition provided a framework in which interior design ideas could be tried out on a temporary basis, and though the installations were indeed temporary, they were executed with all the lavishness and forethought of permanent creations. Exhibition work was the perfect forum for a *Gesamtkunstwerk*, with the architectural setting and accouterments deliberately calculated to complement the art (fine and applied) on display. Again here, the Österreichisches Museum für Kunst und Industrie must be cited as a forerunner, having introduced the practice of displaying objects in roomlike settings as early as 1871. Hoffmann and Moser, the two principal designers of the Secession's early exhibitions, merely took this idea one step further, clarifying and simplifying the presentation so that furniture and art exerted a unified effect. Moser, by training a painter, had a professional understanding of the painter's requirements, and his genius consisted in allowing the works of art to speak for themselves. Gone were the cluttered installations of times past; as Hermann Bahr put it, "He alone, in Central Europe, taught people how to hang pictures."[20] In the "Yellow Room" that Moser designed for the Secession's fifth exhibition, a raised wall frieze (anticipating, significantly, Mackintosh's contribution to the eighth exhibition) served to unify the exhibited works (fig. 62). An even more austere scheme of gray geometric wall stencils was used for Klimt's exhibition four years later. "Nobody understands as he does how to impart the greatest degree of effect to a picture within a given space," wrote Bertha Zuckerkandl of

60. Adolf Loos.

61. Josef Hoffmann. Austrian pavilion at the Deutscher Werkbund exhibition, Cologne. 1913–14.

61

Moser.[21] Klimt agreed and often asked Moser to design his installations.

Of all the early Secession exhibitions, the grandest by far was the so-called Beethoven exhibition of 1902, arranged to honor a single work: Max Klinger's statue of the composer (fig. 63). Klinger's sculpture apparently provided the Secessionists with the incentive to attempt something that had been on their minds for some time. As they noted in the catalogue:

> In the summer of last year, our association decided to interrupt the routine, recurring painting exhibitions with an installation of a different kind. If so far most of these exhibitions had attempted to harmoniously assemble differing components by giving them a unifying connection, and thereby facilitated artistic and modern installation methods, this time we wanted to completely alter the method. A unified room would first be created, and then painting and sculpture would be added to conform to the concept of the room. The idea is to subordinate the parts of the conception to the whole through prescribed relationships and narrowly defined boundaries.... All of these requirements were fulfilled by the task of creating a monumental artwork, and the highest and best that mankind through the ages could offer developed therefrom: the art of the temple.[22]

Olbrich had already conceived of the Secession building as a temple to art, and its movable walls and partitions facilitated the preparation of customized installations. Now the Secessionists decided to carry this idea to its logical conclusion. Gustav Mahler, who in 1902 had just married Carl Moll's stepdaughter, Alma Schindler, was persuaded to create a special arrangement of Beethoven's Ninth Symphony for the occasion. Klimt interpreted the symphony in a monumental frieze that, harking back to Moser's and Mackintosh's innovations, was mounted high on the wall, just below the ceiling. Hoffmann's plan for the exhibition (which separated the frieze from the sculpture to give each maximum impact)

led the visitor in a carefully prescribed circular path whose focus, the Klinger, was unavoidable (fig. 65). The coordination of all the elements, including the incidental furniture and specially designed wall ornaments, all focusing on a single theme, may be judged one of the high points in the realization of the *Gesamtkunstwerk* concept. When complemented by Mahler's music, the exhibition became a performance event that in some ways anticipated the conceptual art of the 1960s and 1970s.

As indicated by the Secessionists' own description of the Beethoven exhibition, it was unique even within the context of that organization's activities. Usually installations were geared to the work of the artists in question, and not vice versa. After the *Klimtgruppe* left the Secession in 1905, nothing quite on the scale of the Beethoven show was ever again attempted, though exhibitions of the more conventional sort continued to be mounted regularly. Exhibitions were part of the routine whereby Austrian wares were shown off both at home and abroad, and Hoffmann, whose knack for such things had been generally acknowledged ever since his prizewinning contributions to the Paris World's Fair in 1900, was kept busy coordinating presentations for the Kunstgewerbeschule, the government and the Wiener Werkstätte. In addition to designing temporary installations for special events (fig. 67), he also coordinated the decor for the Werkstätte's various branches and shops. Before the war, the most important Austrian exhibition project was undoubtedly the 1908 Kunstschau (figs. 68 and 69), the first roundup of avant-garde art organized since the Secession split. However, just as the building itself introduced a new and somewhat reactionary phase in Hoffmann's work, the interior, too, was not entirely up to his usual standard. With his increasingly hectic schedule, the architect had parceled out parts of the assignment to his various Kunstgewerbeschule students, and the whole lacked the unity of conception that had characterized Hoffmann's earlier installations. The Kunstschau may also have simply been too vast to lend itself to a singular vision. It encompassed a garden, a theater and a café; among its dis-

62. Koloman Moser. "Yellow Room," designed for the fifth Secession exhibition. 1899.

62

63

64

ORIENTIERUNGS-
PLAN FÜR DIE
WANDMALEREIEN
UND PLASTIKEN.

65

63. Josef Hoffmann. Beethoven exhibition, Secession;
central room containing
Klinger's sculpture. 1902.

64. Alfred Roller. Poster for
the Beethoven exhibition.
1902. Color lithograph printed

by Albert Berger. 37⅝" × 24¾".

65. Josef Hoffmann. Beethoven exhibition; plan with
Klinger's statue of the composer in the center, and
Klimt's frieze in the room to
the left. 1902.

plays were a mock church and a mock cemetery, in addition to all the bits and baubles of contemporary fine and applied art. Certainly it was endeavoring to be a little world unto itself, but like the real world that it approximated in microcosm, it was pulled in too many distinct directions to be successful as a *Gesamtkunstwerk*.

There were other reasons why the exhibition as *Gesamtkunstwerk* never again reached the perfection represented by the Beethoven show, not the least of which was the utilitarian context which the Wiener Werkstätte by definition gave to its displays. Architectural interiors for private customers were the business only of those who paid for them, but exhibitions were subject to general scrutiny and therefore to general standards. One of the first such enterprises to excite the ire of the press was the *Gedeckte Tisch* (Laid Table) exhibition with which the Wiener Werkstätte inaugurated its Neustiftgasse showroom in 1906. The theme of the exhibition, which was inspired by a similar presentation organized by Eduard Leisching in Brünn (now Brno) the previous year, gave the Werkstätte the ideal opportunity to display its full line of products, from furniture to tablecloths, china, glassware, cutlery, and even flower arrangements. Each table was arrayed according to a particular theme: for example, a wedding (fig. 66), a children's party, a birthday, an artists' gathering. Moser

66

66. Josef Hoffmann. "Wedding Table" designed for the exhibition *Der gedeckte Tisch* (The Laid Table). 1906.

67. Josef Hoffmann. Wiener Werkstätte exhibition, Mannheim. 1907. To the right, Gustav Klimt's *Portrait of Adele Bloch-Bauer I* is flanked by two sculptures by Georg Minne.

67

68. Emil Hoppe. Pavilion designed by Josef Hoffmann for the 1908 Kunstschau; garden façade. Color lithograph postcard (No. 2). 3½" × 5½". Published by the Wiener Werkstätte.

69. Berthold Löffler. Display of contemporary graphics designed for the 1908 Kunstschau.

68

69

70. Alfred Roller. Costume design for a Hofmannsthal-Strauss opera. 1910. Color lithograph. 18¾″ × 12⅝″. Printed by Adolph Fürstner.

had even invented special pastries for the occasion, prompting one reviewer to comment that the only thing fit for consumption at the black and white birthday table would be designer-coordinated poppyseed noodles. Of the wedding table the same critic commented, "Here is where lunacy marries geometry."[23] If the *Gesamtkunstwerk* idea seemed ill-suited to the everyday requirements of eating at table, it also contradicted some of the more practical functions of an exhibition display. The Beethoven exhibition had served one god—art—but most of Hoffmann's later exhibitions were supposed to serve commerce, and sometimes art got in the way. This was one of the many criticisms hurled at Hoffmann's installation for the 1925 Art Deco exhibition: the floor-to-ceiling showcases were monotonous and obscured the goods inside.

THEATER

Given the theatricality of Wiener Werkstätte interiors, and also the relationship between the *Gesamtkunstwerk* and opera, it is surprising that stage design forms a relatively minor, though not unimportant, subcategory of the Werkstätte's sphere of activities. Perhaps the most famous stage designer of the period, Alfred Roller, was only peripherally associated with the Werkstätte. A founding member of the Secession (and from 1909 director of the Kunstgewerbeschule), Roller, who had no prior stage experience, was drawn into the field through his association with Moll and Moll's stepdaughter, Alma Mahler. Gustav Mahler, the controversial director of the Vienna Opera, and Roller formed an ideal team, and after the initial success of Roller's sets for *Tristan und Isolde*, Mahler was even able to lure him away from the Kunstgewerbeschule temporarily to serve as the opera's design director. Both Mahler and Roller believed in the Wagnerian ideal of unifying the various art forms that constitute opera behind a single motivating conception. Roller put forth this conception in his costumes (fig. 70), sets and lighting, which were all tuned to reflect the singular mood of the work in question. "For me the set must be constructed only out of *essentials*," Roller explained, "which do not represent the setting, but which must above all be conditioned by the purpose, like the words or the tempo."[24] This was a variation of functionalism with an artistic, rather than a utilitarian, goal.

Even before Roller's foray into stage design, Moser had a brief association with the ill-fated Jung Wiener Theater zum Lieben Augustin in 1901 (fig. 71). Though no photographic record of Moser's work for this theater survives, contemporary descriptions suggest that it was, for its time, fairly radical. In addition to designing the sets, Moser coordinated related elements such as the curtain in order to break out of the conventional illusionism of the stage and create a suprareal, self-contained world for the actors to inhabit. After the Jung Wiener Theater folded, it would be seven years before Moser returned to stage design, and when he did, his work was far more firmly circumscribed by boundaries of accepted practice. He designed costumes for the dancer Gertrude Bar-

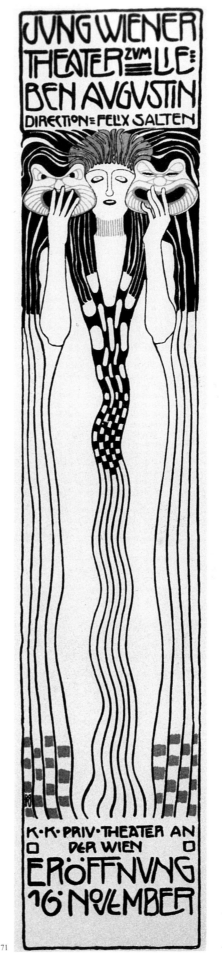

71. Koloman Moser. Poster for the *Jung Wiener Theater zum Lieben Augustin*. 1901.

71

rison and exhibited some stage designs, together with Roller, Czeschka and Emil Orlik, at the 1908 Kunstschau, but his first big opportunity came in 1910, when he was commissioned to oversee a performance of Julius Bittner's *Der Musikant* (The Musician) at the Vienna Opera. The success of this collaboration led to a second opportunity to work with Bittner the following year, on *Der Bergsee* (The Mountain Lake). However, while Moser did sketches for additional projects in the following years, he turned his full attention to painting and no further stage works were realized.

Like Roller, Moser when creating a costume drama was less concerned with the historical accuracy of his renderings than with their overall impact and relationship to the author/composer's conception. "The atmosphere of the set must emphatically mirror the mood produced by the piece," Moser explained. "Whether it is 'plausible,' in the sense of a real-life situation, or 'correct' in the sense of a particular period, is a less important consideration. It must above all be at one with the poetry."[25] Unlike Wagner, Moser felt that each of the components of a *Gesamtkunstwerk* must abandon its individual identity to achieve a new, integral identity within the context of the work. In this, his thinking was already very close to that of Kandinsky and the pioneers of expressionist drama, but it would take this next generation to explore the fullest implications of the *Gesamtkunstwerk* as theater.

The artists of the Wiener Werkstätte and their contemporaries remained too much concerned with spectacle, too little interested in expression. It is ironic that many of the leading artists of this period, who had struggled so hard to throw off the residue of historicism, participated in the preparation of a mammoth *Festzug*, à la Makart, to honor the sixtieth anniversary of the emperor's coronation in 1908. Although Hoffmann resigned from the parade committee when it rejected his preliminary sketches, the Kunstschau was itself part of the general festivities. Moser, no longer officially associated with the Wiener Werkstätte, designed a best-selling commemorative postcard for the Staatsdruckerei (State Printing Press), and the Werkstätte issued its own group of annivsary postcards (pls. 9 and 10). The *Festzug*, which required all manner of historical costumes as well as a variety of printed matter, energized the entire artistic community. Insofar as its involvement with theater proper was concerned, the Wiener Werkstätte seems chiefly to have contributed costume designs, and these mainly after the founding of the fashion division in 1910 or 1911. For contemporary dramas and comedies, current styles were appropriate, and the Werkstätte encouraged actresses to promote the latest line by giving them discounts. Special outfits were also created for costume dramas, and the Wiener Werkstätte regularly designed costumes for Grete Wiesenthal and a number of other dancers.

The Wiener Werkstätte's most significant theatrical performance, true to form, was not presented behind the curtain, but in front of it. The project was the interior of the Cabaret Fledermaus (or "Bat," after the popular operetta of the same name), a brainchild of Fritz Wärndorfer that opened in the autumn of 1907 (figs. 72 and 73). This was a *Gesamtkunstwerk* in the grand Wiener Werkstätte tradition,

with an all-star cast of characters that included Czeschka, Hoffmann, Kokoschka, Löffler, Moser, Orlik and Wimmer, as well as literary collaborators such as Bahr and Peter Altenberg. Hoffmann, in addition to supervising the architectural details and designing the famous black and white "Fledermaus chairs" (fig. 76), also put his hand to posters, stage sets and costumes. The Wiener Keramik provided the colorful tiles for the bar area (pl. 7). Though the Cabaret Fledermaus was created as a gathering place for the avantgarde of the day (something that may have contributed to its precarious finances),[26] the experience it sought to provide was decidedly sensual, not spiritual. The Fledermaus's statement of purpose (even a brothel, in these days, must have required a manifesto) was very clear on this point: "We believe that with an aesthetically impeccable design of the scene only half of what we desire has been achieved … we have considered it important … to turn our artistic attention with as much love to the most inconsiderable as to what is great: the interior design just as the table silver, the light fixtures just as the smallest utensils thus have sprung from the unified basic concept of the room to be created, not forgetting the care for the practical and hygienic needs of the audience … pure air controlled in temperature, a cultivated cuisine, the totality of comfortable seating and agreeable service belong here."[27] The Cabaret Fledermaus, with its American bartender and French chef, was not a place to rock one out of one's complacency. This was not a *Gesamtkunstwerk* that would reach far beyond the realm of ordinary experience, but rather one that would meet the audience at its own level and smother it with its effusive aesthetics. An environment like that of the Cabaret Fledermaus deliberately blurred the distinction between the activities taking place on each side of the stage.

FURNITURE

Crucial to all the Wiener Werkstätte's interior design work—whether undertaken for a cabaret, an exhibition or a home—was, of course, the furniture. Not only was the furniture the major element in the composition of any interior, but it is through its furniture designs that the Wiener Werkstätte is best known to us today. The furniture has survived long after the interiors for which it was created have been dismantled or overhauled, and unlike the smaller Werkstätte decorative objects, it is capable of establishing a commanding presence in a modern room.

From the start, Hoffmann and Moser worked in close cooperation with the existing furniture industry in Austria. Such collaboration between artists and craftsmen (which would find its ultimate realization in the Wiener Werkstätte) had long been fostered by the Österreichisches Museum für Kunst und Industrie and the Kunstgewerbeschule. While the Wiener Werkstätte work program railed against the proliferation of mass-produced goods and shoddy workmanship, the better furniture factories in Austria were largely immune from this tendency. Craftsmanship was essential for the production of a fine piece of furniture, and even if certain subordinate tasks were carried out with the aid of machinery or

72

73

74   75

72. Josef Hoffmann. Cabaret
Fledermaus, Vienna; bar-
room with tiles produced by
the Wiener Keramik. 1907.

73. Josef Hoffmann. Cabaret
Fledermaus; theater and dining room. 1907.

74. Josef Hoffmann. Table
lamp designed for the Cabaret
Fledermaus. 1907. Painted
metal and fabric, with glass
inserts. Approximately 12″
high. Executed by the Wiener
Werkstätte.

75. Berthold Löffler. Sketch
for an envelope for the Cabaret Fledermaus (detail). 1908.
Ink and pencil. Signed "K.
Moser" in pencil, lower right,
but printed with Löffler's
initials.

76. Josef Hoffmann. Variation on a chair designed for
the Cabaret Fledermaus.
After 1907. Painted beechwood. 28½″ high. Executed by
Jacob & Josef Kohn.

76

77

77. Gustav Siegel. Display
designed for Jacob & Josef
Kohn at the Paris World's Fair.
1900. Siegel's chair became
the prototype for Otto
Wagner's better-known Postsparkasse chair (see fig. 12).

78. Michael Thonet. Chair designed for the Palais Liechtenstein, Vienna. 1843-46. Gilt beechwood with upholstered seat. 35⅜" high.

79. Michael Thonet. Chair Number 14. 1859. Stained beechwood with caned seat. 36⅜" high.

80. Adolf Loos. Chair designed for the Café Museum, Vienna. 1898. Stained beechwood with caned seat. 34¼" high. Executed by Gebrüder Thonet.

delegated to assistants, a skilled master still supervised the construction of each item from start to finish. The Wiener Werkstätte, at least until 1908, employed its own cabinetmakers, but it, or its designers, also collaborated with independent craftsmen and the better furniture factories, such as Portois & Fix. While it is understandable that the Werkstätte designers would require the assistance of outside firms, the enthusiasm with which Hoffmann, Moser and the others embraced the bentwood technology of such enterprises as Gebrüder Thonet and Jacob & Josef Kohn is surprising. For the bentwood factories were the chief exception to the rule: the one branch of the Austrian furniture industry that had wholeheartedly endorsed mass production.

The process of "bending wood in acute angles, permitting the production of new shapes"[28] was perfected by Michael Thonet between 1830 and 1850. The methodology itself dates back to the early years of the nineteenth century, when it was used principally to facilitate the construction of round parts such as wheels. Thonet, a cabinetmaker originally based in Boppard on the Rhine, refined the technology so that it could be used for the manufacture of furniture. At the invitation of no less a personage than Prince Metternich, he brought his invention to Vienna in 1842 and almost immediately received the prestigious assignment to assist in the furnishing of the Palais Liechtenstein. The so-called Liechtenstein chair, designed between 1843 and 1846, became the classic Thonet prototype (fig. 78). One can imagine that it required its original coat of gilt to appear suitably dressed up in the elegant palace, for otherwise it was a model of simplicity. Its clean lines represented the best of late Biedermeier design, and its unity of form and construction led directly to the modernist innovations of the early twentieth century. While Gebrüder Thonet (the "Gebrüder," or brothers, were actually the founder's sons) embraced the prevalent historicist fad after Michael's death in 1871, Adolf Loos, in furnishing his Café Museum,

revived the austere, earlier designs and adapted them for his own chair (fig. 80).

Modern design and technology married happily in the bentwood furniture industry. After Michael Thonet's original patent expired in 1869, others were free to enter the market, and by the turn of the century the firm of Jacob & Josef Kohn had become Thonet's most serious competitor. At least in the beginning, competition appears to have hurt neither firm either economically or artistically.[29] By 1904, Thonet could boast no fewer than seven factories in various parts of the empire; Kohn, in 1907, had six thousand employees producing seven thousand pieces a day. The enormous success of the bentwood industry, abroad as well as at home (80 percent of Kohn's output was exported), was made possible by the ease and cheapness of the technique. No master craftsmen were required here; simple glue and screws held the pieces together and made repairs equally effortless. Thonet's best-selling "Chair Number 14" was composed of six basic wooden parts and ten screws (fig. 79). The bentwood industry was among the most technologically advanced in Vienna at the turn of the century, and it quickly became one of the most artistically sophisticated as well. Just before the turn of

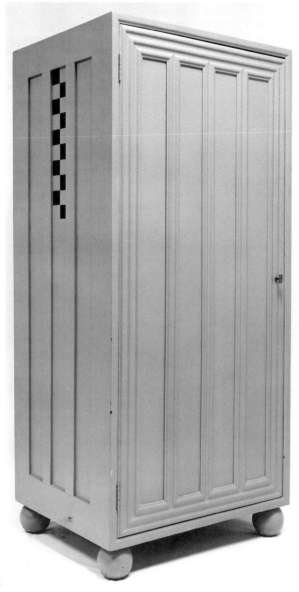

81

83

81. Koloman Moser. Cabinet. 1904. White and gray painted oak. 58¾″ high. Executed by the Wiener Werkstätte.

82. Koloman Moser. Proportion study for a bench. 1904. Tempera and pencil. Designed for an "Apartment for a Young Couple."

83. Koloman Moser. Writing desk and chair. 1903–04. Ebony and boxwood. 56¾″ high. Executed by the Wiener Werkstätte for Fritz Wärndorfer's mother.

the century, Kohn appointed Gustav Siegel, a former Hoffmann student, as its artistic adviser. When a chair that Siegel designed (and which became the progenitor of Wagner's Postsparkasse chair [fig. 12]) won first prize at the Paris World's Fair in 1900 (fig. 77), the the implications were clear for all to see. Artists' names, mentioned by Kohn in its ads, became in and of themselves a selling point. The age of designer furniture had come to Vienna, and Thonet quickly joined the trend by producing items by Loos, Wagner, Hoffmann, Moser and others. The speed with which the various furniture firms rushed to embrace "modern" design in the early years of the twentieth century also encouraged its share of inferior "knockoffs." This, and the fact that even the genuine designer pieces were often produced in multiple variations, sometimes makes it difficult to arrive at firm attributions.

Hoffmann laid out his basic tenets of furniture design in a 1901 essay, "Simple Furniture," published in *Das Interieur*. Furniture, he believed, should above all be functional and demonstrate integrity of both material and execution. Therefore, with the exception of bentwood, furniture should not employ curved shapes, for the only honorable way to achieve such effects would be "to go into the forest to look for the correctly curved branch."[30] Angularity was more in keeping with the intrinsic nature of wood and the techniques of joinery. Freestanding pieces, Hoffmann continued, ought to be inherently distinct from built-in units: "Style ... must make a principle apparent, so that we can distinguish between a board, a pillar, and a case piece." Insofar as the decoration of wooden objects was concerned, Hoffmann felt that no wood should be stained to resemble another, but that it was permissible to paint or stain pieces to obtain a color not found in

84. Josef Hoffmann. Settee. Ca. 1904. Painted beechwood with upholstered seat and back. 30″ high. Executed by Gebrüder Thonet.

85. Josef Hoffmann. Chair. Ca. 1908. Stained beech with brass fittings and upholstered seat, back and arms. 29¼″ high. Executed by Jacob & Josef Kohn.

86. Josef Hoffmann. "Egg" rocking chair. 1905. Stained beechwood. 47¼″ long. Executed by Jacob & Josef Kohn.

nature. The unusual colors used for much modern furniture and interiors at the turn of the century—green, gray, blue, violet and red were especially popular—often faded quickly, and unlike the more familiar black and white pieces of later years, these innovations have today been largely forgotten. As to more complex surface ornamentation, such as carvings or intarsia, Hoffmann remained ambivalent. Unless such artistically conceived designs could be adequately conveyed to the craftsman or, better still, executed by the designer himself, they probably ought to be avoided. Similarly, intricate inlays on ornamental panels that were not integral to the overall construction of the piece represented a conflict of purpose.

With Hoffmann's proscriptions on curves and decorative detailing—two of the chief components of *Jugendstil* design—the flowering of Art Nouveau was effectively curtailed, at least as it concerned the avant-garde. Of the Wiener Werkstätte's two leaders, it was Moser, the quintessential graphic artist, who made the more extensive use of decora-

tive inlays and panels in his furniture (pls. 13 and 14). As a painter, he was geared to thinking in two dimensions and was better able to grasp the geometric implications of such formative influences as *Jugendstil* or Art Nouveau. What he lacked, however, was Hoffmann's firm understanding of the principles of three-dimensional construction, and Moser's furniture designs, so pretty on paper (fig. 82), often appear boxy and awkward when executed (fig. 81). Perhaps his best known exhibition piece—a buffet called the "Miraculous Draught of Fishes" first shown at the eighth Secession exhibition of 1900—is most commendable for the graphic originality of the inlaid design from which it takes its name; its neo-Biedermeier bulk, however, is rather overwhelming. Moser's furniture, at the time, was criticized for being too self-consciously artistic; such things, sniffed one critic, "are not merely made, but ... born."[31]

Hoffmann so loved square and cubic forms that he earned the nickname *Quadratl* (Little Square), but Moser was equally fond of such geometric devices, and it may even be that he, through his graphic arts connections, first brought them to the collaboration. As Bahr noted, "For the Viennese, Moser was the man of little squares, and most people thought he must have invented the chessboard."[32] Nonetheless, Moser's forms were somehow softer and less uncompromising than Hoffmann's, more "feminine" in the stereotypical sense of the word. As Klimt supposedly noted, "If one wants to see at once which [pieces] are by Hoffmann and which by Moser, one needs only to look at who is standing in front of them. All the women are attracted to Moser, the men stream to Hoffmann."[33] Moser's approach remained essentially decorative, sidestepping the seamless welding of form and construction that was Hoffmann's forte.

Perhaps the piece of furniture that best sums up Hoffmann's philosophy is the *Sitzmaschine* (machine for sitting) (pl. 16). Originally designed for the Purkersdorf Sanatorium in 1904 or 1905, the chair, like so many of Hoffmann's creations, was eventually manufactured in a variety of finishes and with various different seats and backs. In its combination of flat and bent wood, lines and curves, the chair represents a concise glossary of Hoffmann's formal vocabulary. Its original purpose—a reclining chair for convalescents—and the literal meaning of its name reflect the designer's professed functionalism and even his latent admiration of the "machine" as an embodiment of that functionalism. Yet as anyone who has ever sat in one can confirm, the *Sitzmaschine* is less a machine for sitting than a beautiful piece of sculpture. As was so often the case, Hoffmann was torn between the practical and the beautiful. Of his three ideals—form, construction and function—function was the first to be sacrificed in favor of the other two.

METALWORK

The metal shop was the first of the Wiener Werkstätte's various divisions to operate, as it was to metalwork that the Werkstätte's first provisional apartment space had been devoted. Hoffmann and Moser produced some of their most innovative early designs in metal, and here, as elsewhere, their collaboration is so close that often only signed (usually silver) pieces can be attributed with any degree of certainty. Silver, less costly and tougher than gold, figured prominently in the metal shop's output, though the Werkstätte also produced pieces in brass, silver plate (*Alpaka*) and enameled metal, sometimes in combination with other substances such as wood, ivory or semiprecious stones. Metal may be considered the base material for many of the utilitarian objects, such as lighting fixtures (fig. 99), lamps, candelabra, clocks (fig. 97), bowls (pl. 18, fig. 95), boxes (pls. 4 and 5, fig. 94), vases (pl. 17) and planters, that were required to properly fit out a Werkstätte interior. Three basic types of objects, however, seem to dominate the early metal designs of the Werkstätte: hammered vessels and boxes, flatware (figs. 87, 88, 90 and 92), and the ubiquitous *Gitterwerk* (latticework) (figs. 89 and 91).

Gitterwerk is the name given to a host of different objects manufactured from sheet metal perforated by a regular pattern of squares. The use of cut or incised squares as decorative motifs (often within flat expanses, such as chair backs) had been pioneered by Mackintosh, but it took the Wiener Werkstätte's *Gitterwerk* to incorporate this motif as an integral structural component. The appeal of this iconography to both "*Quadratl*" Hoffmann and his collaborator Moser is obvious, and it is impossible to determine which of the two men actually invented the process. The *Gitterwerk* was one of the first types of objects to be offered for sale in the Werkstätte's shops, and its frequent inclusion in articles on the Werkstätte made it something of a "signature" item. Adding to this was the enormous versatility of the technique, which could be adapted to the manufacture of almost any sort of container, and the fact that it could be made to suit various budgets, either in sterling or painted metal. *Gitterwerk* was one of the many early Werkstätte products that could easily have been adapted for mass production, and in fact after 1910 it was manufactured by the firm of Cloeter.

Of all the metal objects designed by the Wiener Werkstätte, tableware must be considered by nature the most functional. Unlike a box or a vase, which can be put to use or not at the owner's discretion (and if not, remains attractive as an ornament in the room), flatware must, first and foremost, be usable for eating. Whether the flatware designed by Hoffmann, Czeschka, Prutscher, Wimmer and Zimpel over the years fulfilled this basic criterion is debatable. Certainly the treatment of knives, forks and spoons as miniature sculpture might have done little to sate one's hunger, but it did a lot to satisfy Hoffmann's taste for geometric experimentation. Two basic Hoffmann designs are identifiable: the "flat model," originally produced in 1903 or 1904 for Fritz Wärndorfer (fig. 90), and the "round model," based on the cutlery designed for the Palais Stoclet (fig. 92). Although Hoffmann created more flatware designs for the Wiener Werkstätte than anyone else, dating and attribution are as difficult here as in other areas of the Werkstätte's activities. Hoffmann sometimes initialed sketches that he had, in fact, only corrected for others, while artists who adapted Hoffmann's designs nonetheless retained the master's initials. Designs that were originally created for specific clients were later put into general production and turned out in myriad variations over the course of the years. The range of objects thus runs the gamut from unique pieces—often with richly decorated handles of carved wood or ivory—to items that were more or less mass produced. Between 1907 and 1909, and possibly also later on, the firm of Bachmann & Co. manufactured much of the silver plate.

The other metal objects produced and/or designed by the Wiener Werkstätte ranged from very simple to highly elaborate, from the hammered silver and silver-plate boxes (fig. 94) that provide a cubic counterpart to the *Gitterwerk* squares, to ornate tea services and samovars (fig. 93). The metal objects reflect the same general stylistic trends that are observed in other areas of Viennese design. Early pieces (including some done by Olbrich before he left Vienna) reveal the waning influence of Art Nouveau, which was soon supplanted by the constructivist/geometric phase of Hoffmann's and Moser's collaborative years. Later a resurgence of more elaborate decorative schemes was expressed both in the surface ornamentation of the metalwork and in the over-

87. Josef Hoffmann. Decorative spoons. Ca. 1905–06. Silver and semiprecious stones. Executed by the Wiener Werkstätte.

88. Josef Hoffmann. Two forks. Ca. 1923–24. Silver. These forks are typical of a pattern originally designed for the Primavesi family and often embellished with the owner's initials or a decorative motif.

89. Two *Tafelaufsätze* (centerpieces) and a basket. White painted sheet iron. Each approximately 5″ high. Executed by the Wiener Werkstätte.

90. Josef Hoffmann. Tableware: "Flat Model." Ca. 1904. Silver. Designed for Lilly and Fritz Wärndorfer and executed by the Wiener Werkstätte.

91. Koloman Moser. Bud vase. 1905. Silver. 8½″ high. Executed by the Wiener Werkstätte.

92. Josef Hoffmann. Tableware: "Round Model." Ca. 1906. Silver. Executed by the Wiener Werkstätte. This tableware was designed for the Palais Stoclet and also used by Friederika Maria Beer, Sonja Knips, Magda Mautner-Markhof, and Hoffmann himself.

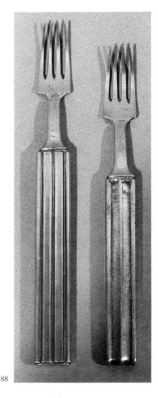

87

88

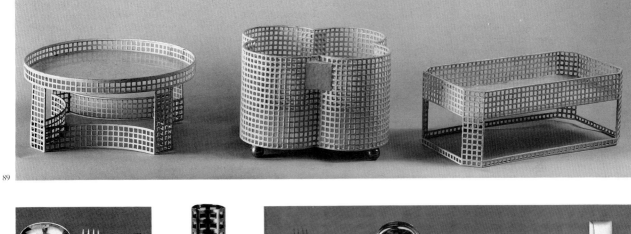

89

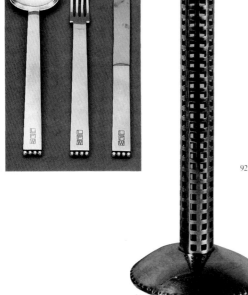

90

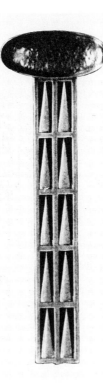

91

92

93

93. Josef Hoffmann. Samovar. 1909–10. Silver and ivory. 11⅜″ high. Executed by the Wiener Werkstätte.

94. Josef Hoffmann. Box. Ca. 1903. Silver plate. 4″ high. Executed by Josef Berger for the Wiener Werkstätte.

95. Josef Hoffmann. Bowl. Ca. 1904. Silver. 2¼″ high. Executed by the Wiener Werkstätte.

96. Berthold Löffler. Sketch for a clock. Ink, pencil and crayon on paper. Inscribed, upper and lower margins. 5½″ × 8¾″.

97. Josef Hoffmann. Clock. Ca. 1910–12. Silvered metal.

98. Koloman Moser. Vase. 1903. Brass and semiprecious stones. 12¼″ high. Executed by Karl Kallert for the Wiener Werkstätte.

99. Dagobert Peche. Lamp. 1918. Metal and fabric. 47½″ high. Executed by the Wiener Werkstätte.

94

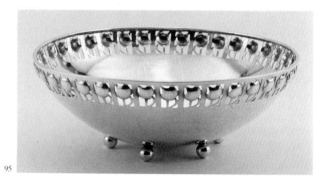

95

96

97

98

99

100

all shapes of objects: sinuous handles and curved, fluted bowls (pl. 18). Particular mention must be made, in this regard, of the fantastic silver creations designed by Dagobert Peche around 1920 (figs. 147 and 150). To say that these contradict the reductive simplicity of the earlier boxes and *Gitterwerk* almost misses the point, for the Peche pieces have altogether abandoned any pretense of functionalism. They are, in fact, not works of applied art at all, but sculptures in their own right. Craft has, in these objects, become art.

GLASS

Unlike metal objects, glass was never manufactured by the Wiener Werkstätte. Perhaps because its production required complex facilities and technology, and because both the glass and ceramics industries were traditionally based in Bohemia and Moravia, it proved easier to license much of this work to outside firms for production. In the production of glass, two firms—Bakalowits and Lobmeyr—stood in much the same relationship to each other as did Kohn and Thonet in the field of bentwood furniture. Bakalowits took the lead in establishing ties with avant-garde artist/designers (in particular, with Moser and his students), and Lobmeyr later attempted to catch up by collaborating with the Wiener Werkstätte. Moser had begun working with glass in 1898, and the following year he won an award for a glass service pro-

101

100. Koloman Moser and Robert Holubetz. Vases. Ca. 1900–01. Green iridescent glass. Executed by E. Bakalowits Söhne.

101. Josef Hoffmann. Two vases. Ca. 1920. Glass. 4⅛″ and 5⅞″ high. Executed by J. & L. Lobmeyr.

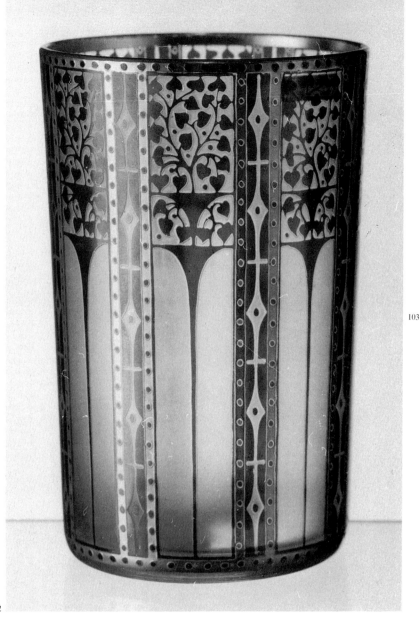

102

103

102. Josef Hoffmann.
Glass. Ca. 1910–11.
Decorated with gold and
bronzite. 4⅛″ high. Executed
via J. & L. Lobmeyr for the
Wiener Werkstätte.

103. Josef Hoffmann (glass)
and Ludwig Heinrich Jung-
nickel (decoration). Sketch
for a wineglass. Ca. 1910–18.
Executed by J. & L. Lobmeyr.

duced by Bakalowits. Bakalowits went on to garner another prize for Moser's work in Paris the following year, thereby solidifying the collaboration. Moser's glass designs revealed an intuitive understanding of the material that allowed his ornamental flare to be incorporated in the structure of each piece with seemingly effortless simplicity. As Art Nouveau faded and the push toward simplicity became stronger, many designs were executed in a variety of finishes in order to please different tastes, with Loetz specializing in the more old-fashioned iridescent vases (pl. 12). Moser is credited with pioneering (though initially without much success) a shift to black and white glassware, or "Zebraware," in 1903. Such motifs would first become truly popular a few years later, when they turn up both in Hoffmann's glassware and in the ceramic glazes of the Wiener Keramik (figs. 102, 106, 107 and 108).

In 1910 Bakalowits's rival, Lobmeyr, executed its first designs by Hoffmann. Often Hoffmann designed only the basic form, and another artist supplied the decoration (fig. 103). The Wiener Werkstätte started purchasing plain glass and adding its own hand-painted decorations in 1915 (pls. 23 and 24); glass-cutting equipment was acquired in 1919. Whereas the etching sometimes had to be done by trained craftsmen after prepared sketches, the painting was usually done directly by such artists as Peche, Hoffmann, Mathilde Flögl, Hilda Jesser, Fritzi Löw, Vally Wieselthier and Julius Zimpel. Around 1920, Hoffmann also began designing a series of rather solid-looking vessels of cut colored glass (pl. 21). These objects, which derived their effect from the color and cut of the glass rather than from surface decoration, employ fluted and rounded shapes analogous to those seen in Hoffmann's metalwork from this period.

104. Jutta Sika. Coffee service. Ca. 1901–02. Porcelain with stenciled decoration. Approximately 2½″ to 7¾″ high. Executed by Josef Böck.

105. School of Koloman Moser. Plate. 1901–02. Ceramic. 9⅝″ in diameter.   104

CERAMICS

In the field of ceramics, as in so many others, the Österreichisches Museum für Kunst und Industrie and the Kunstgewerbeschule led the way in forging ties between artists and industry, both through the exhibition of exemplary works and by fostering collaboration between student designers and craftsmen. The district technical schools, or *Fachschulen*, served as satellites of the Kunstgewerbeschule, linking it with developments in the provinces and vice versa. The Kunstgewerbeschule's chemical laboratory complemented the artistic innovations of its design departments with technical research, and in 1900 a course in ceramics techniques was incorporated in the curriculum. Hoffmann and Moser gave the young ceramicists formal instruction, and the ceramicists, in turn, executed designs produced by Moser's and Hoffmann's regular students. Moser was especially active in forming ties with the ceramics industry, and his students reaped the benefits of these connections. Before long the mark "*Schule Moser*" (School of Moser) became something of a brand name and sign of distinction. The firm of Böck, in particular, demonstrated an unusual willingness to pursue the best in modern design. The early *Schule Moser* ceramics drew their strength from exceedingly pure geometric forms, decorated with equally severe patterns or, in some cases, not decorated at all. Jutta Sika's coffee service may be considered the epitome of this phase (fig. 104).

The founding of the Wiener Keramik by Michael Powolny and Berthold Löffler in 1906 more or less coincides with the end of the Wiener Werkstätte's purist phase, and the consequent resurgence of ornamentalism can be seen in the Wiener Keramik's interest in decorative ceramic sculptures (fig. 107). Curlicues and curves (sometimes tempered by linear geometry or a black and white color scheme), flowers and almost offensively cute putti (fig. 108), were the hallmarks of the Powolny/Löffler style. Powolny had trained as a potter, but Löffler was a graphic designer whose influence was also

105

felt in other items produced by the Werkstätte around this time. After 1907, the Werkstätte began distributing the products of the Wiener Keramik, and as previously discussed, it also hired the firm to provide tiles for the Palais Stoclet and the Cabaret Fledermaus. Although geometric ceramic tiles had been used in Hoffmann interiors as far back as the Hohe Warte villas, the incorporation of more elaborate ceramic insets, like the mosaics of Leopold Forstner's studio, were particularly suited to the new turn to decorative richness. Moser is credited with expanding the vocabulary of mosaicwork by proposing a methodology whereby unconventional materials such as majolica, glass and copper could be embedded in a cement ground.[34] Mosaics and ceramics became a bridge between the fine and the applied arts; they made it possible to elaborate an interior through the incorporation of artistic vignettes, but at the same time they reduced artistic

106

108

109

107

110

106. Michael Powolny and
Berthold Löffler. *Tafelaufsatz*
(centerpiece). Ca. 1906.
Black and white porcelain.
9⅞″ in diameter.

107. Michael Powolny (*left
and right*) and Berthold
Löffler (*center*). Figurine and
candy dishes. Ca. 1912–13.
Black and white glazed
ceramic. Approximately 4¾″
to 8″ high. Executed by the
Wiener Keramik.

108. Michael Powolny.
Planter. Ca. 1911–12. Black
and white ceramic. 9⅜″ high.
Executed by the Wiener
Keramik.

109. Vally Wieselthier. Candelabra. Ca. 1920–25. Glazed
ceramic. 15″ high.

110. Susi Singer. Figurine.
Ca. 1920–25. Glazed painted
ceramic. 16½″ high.

expression to the level of interior decoration.

The merging of art and artifact constituted a moral
dilemma that was to plague the Wiener Werkstätte throughout its later years. Powolny's and Löffler's ceramic figures,
like the silver creatures of Dagobert Peche, were not truly
sculptures in the full, fine-arts sense of the term. Rather, they
occupied an uneasy middle ground: whimsical, decorative,
more or less useless, and not especially profound. When the
Wiener Werkstätte finally geared up to produce its own
ceramics in 1917, this tendency prompted it to concentrate on
the production of unique figurines. Ceramicists such as Susi
Singer (pl. 27, fig. 110), Gudrun Baudisch and Vally Wieselthier (pl. 25) aspired to the status of full-fledged artists. "It
would be quite inadequate," wrote one reviewer, "to label
Susi Singer as no more than a ceramic designer, merely
because clay happens to be her main material.... Her best
pieces achieve total validity as art in the round."[35] Yet charming though the works of Susi Singer and the others may be,
they are *Kleinkunst* in the most literal sense of the word:
"little art" with none of the sweep or majesty of real sculpture, and none of the functional simplicity of earlier Viennese ceramics.

12

12. Koloman Moser. Vase. Ca.
1901. Iridescent glass. 9″ high.
Executed by Johann Loetz
Witwe.

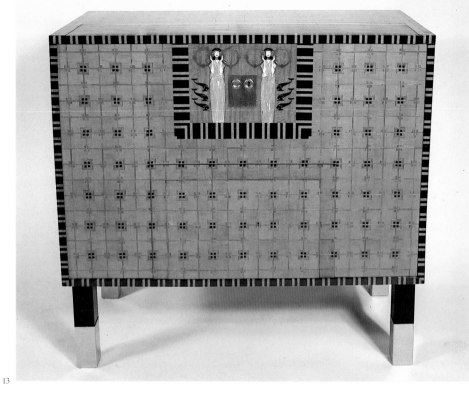

13

13. Koloman Moser. Writing desk. 1903. Elm, rosewood, ebony, mother-of-pearl and ivory. 43¼″ high. Executed by Portois & Fix for the interior of the Charlottenlund Palace in Stockholm.

15. Koloman Moser (attr.). Vitrine. Stained beechwood with brass fittings. 72½″ high. Executed by Jacob & Josef Kohn.

14

15

14. Koloman Moser. Chair. 1904. Cedar and lemonwood. 27½″ high. Designed as part of an "Apartment for a Young Couple" and executed by Kaspar Hrazdil.

16

16. Josef Hoffmann. *Sitzmaschine* (machine for sitting).
1904. Stained beechwood. 38¾″
high. Originally designed for
the Purkersdorf Sanatorium
and later manufactured by
Jacob & Josef Kohn.

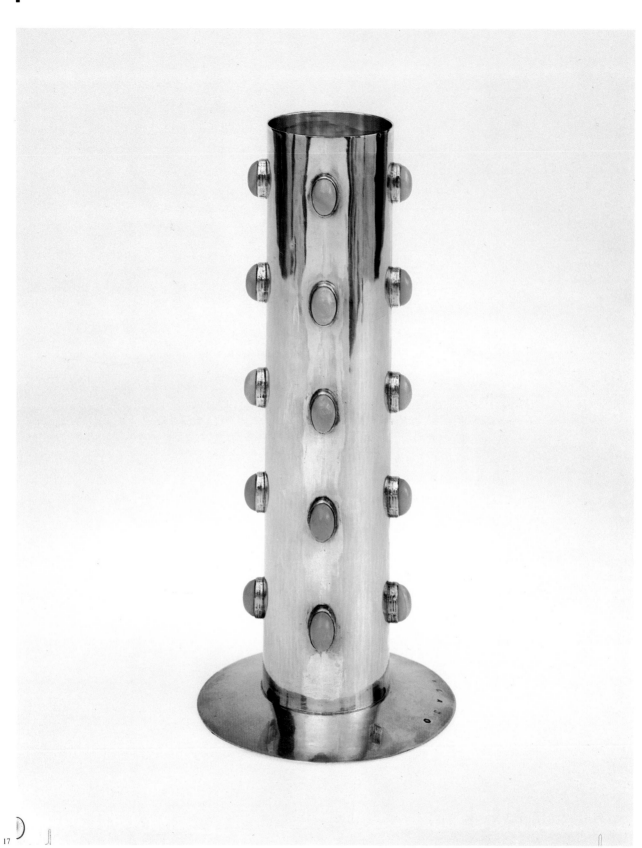

17. Koloman Moser. Vase.
1905. Silver and amber. 8⅝″
high. Executed by Josef Hoss-
feld for the Wiener Werkstätte.

18

19

18. Dagobert Peche. Bowl. Silver. 4″ high. Executed by the Wiener Werkstätte.

19. Josef Hoffmann. *Tafelaufsatz* (centerpiece). 1907. Silver. 5¾″ high. Executed by the Wiener Werkstätte.

20. Otto Prutscher. Wine gob-
let. Ca. 1905. Hand-painted
glass. 8⅛″ high.

21. Josef Hoffmann. Bowl.
Ca. 1920. Blue glass. 4⅞″ high.
Executed by Meyrs Neffe.

22. Dagobert Peche (attr). Jar.
Ca. 1916. Hand-painted glass.
11″ high. Executed by the Wiener Werkstätte.

23

23. Four hand-painted glasses. Ca. 1917–19. Each approximately 5″ high. Executed by the Wiener Werkstätte.

24. Mathilde Flögl (*left and center*) and Vally Wieselthier (*right*). Jar and two goblets. Hand-painted glass. Ca. 1917–19. 10″, 4¾″ and 9¼″ high. Executed (via Oertel/Haida) by the Wiener Werkstätte.

24

25

27

26

28

25. Vally Wieselthier. Figurine. Ca. 1920–25. Glazed blue and orange ceramic. 9½″ high. Executed by the Wiener Werkstätte.

26. Hilda Jesser. Vase. Ca. 1925. Glazed painted ceramic. 9½″ high. Executed by the Wiener Werkstätte.

27. Susi Singer. Figurine. Ca. 1917–20. Glazed painted ceramic. 13¼″ high. Executed by the Wiener Werkstätte.

28. Michael Powolny. Inkwell. Ca. 1908–09. Glazed painted ceramic. 6″ high. Executed by the Wiener Keramik.

FASHION
AND RELATED DEVELOPMENTS

Architecture, interior and display design, furniture, metalwork, glass and ceramics, though not all actually produced by the Wiener Werkstätte, were part of its design program from the beginning. With architecture providing the general framework, the other entities served an accessory function, making possible the creation of a complete living environment in the *Gesamtkunstwerk* mode.

The official opening of the fashion department under the direction of Eduard Josef Wimmer-Wisgrill in 1911, however, constituted a leap into an area of domesticity that had previously been touched but not penetrated by the Wiener Werkstätte. The shift in emphasis from the production of "hard" goods, such as buildings and furniture, to "soft" objects, such as garments and textiles, represented a shift from the grand statement to the ephemeral. In invading the very person of the consumer, the Wiener Werkstätte had hoped to turn this consumer—body and presumably soul—into an art object. Nevertherless, the result was a growing trivialization of art, an increased involvement with all sorts of *Kleinigkeiten* (trifles) such as hats and handbags, belt buckles and bedroom slippers. Therefore, the opening of the fashion department provides a convenient point of departure for a discussion of the later phases of the Wiener Werkstätte and its gradual artistic decline.

CLOTHING DESIGN

Almost from the start, Wiener Werkstätte designers perceived an aesthetic conflict between their carefully coordinated interiors and the totally uncoordinated garments worn by the people who inhabited those interiors. Between 1901 and 1906, Moser designed at least four dresses (pl. 29), and Hoffmann, too, turned his attention to the problem, at least in theory if not in practice.[1] Contact with Klimt, who

111

111. Gustav Klimt. Photograph of Emilie Flöge. Ca. 1903.

113

114

112. Eduard Josef Wimmer-Wisgrill. Hats designed for the Wiener Werkstätte. Ca. 1910.

113. Wiener Werkstätte dress. 1911.

114. Mela Köhler. Wiener Werkstätte dress. 1911. Color lithograph postcard (No. 523). 5½″ × 3½″. Published by the Wiener Werkstätte.

112

designed his own flowing work robes and dresses for his lover, Emilie Flöge (fig. 111), helped to further this impulse. Flöge and her sister ran one of Vienna's leading fashion salons, which had been designed by Hoffmann and Moser in 1904 (fig. 36). Klimt's dress designs were published in *Deutsche Kunst und Dekoration*, as were contemporary German fashions, suggesting that clothing be considered an integral component of the then burgeoning international arts revival. The Cabaret Fledermaus provided the Wiener Werkstätte with practical experience in costume design; a fashion division thus became from many points of view a logical addition to its program.

A firm date for the opening of the Wiener Werkstätte fashion department cannot altogether be established, for it seems likely that the Werkstätte was designing (and probably producing) garments well before it received formal permission to do so on March 9, 1911.[2] Possibly the Flöge salon executed Werkstätte designs during this preliminary period. By 1910, when a collection of hats by Hoffmann and Eduard Wimmer was illustrated in *Deutsche Kunst und Dekoration* (fig. 112), the Wiener Werkstätte was already selling at least a few articles of clothing, and it appears that the idea was first tried out that year at the Karlsbad branch. The "so-called fashion department," headed by Wimmer, who had studied architecture with Hoffmann at the Kunstgewerbeschule, was not very successful initially. Wimmer informed the home office, "We are just barely keeping our heads above water," and continued, "Today I declared ... that I would give up the great hat salon from this time forward, and just stick the winter hats in a chest and try to sell it."[3]

115. Three Wiener Werk-
stätte outfits. 1917.

115

Nonetheless, despite this lack of success, and despite the fact that Wimmer claimed to be fed up with dealing with women and "female junk,"[4] the fashion department went on to settle and even flourish in Vienna under Wimmer's direction.

The first Wiener Werkstätte fashion collection debuted in April 1911, scarcely a month after the department received the official go-ahead. Stylistically, the line incorporated two basic trends: that of the "*Reformkleid*" (reform dress) and its reinterpretation by the French designer Paul Poiret. The *Reformkleid*, a turn-of-the-century invention that followed the rejection of the corset as the foundation of women's fashions, had inspired the caftanlike garments of Klimt and Moser. Though certainly a laudable innovation in both social and health terms, the reform dress was not particularly flattering to the female figure. Bertha Zuckerkandl bluntly

called it a "flour sack."[5] Poiret's contribution was the revival of the Empire waist, which cinched the fabric under the bustline and thereby gave shape to the unwieldy garment. In early Wiener Werkstätte fashion sketches and photos, examples of both the "flour sack" and Empire-waisted models may be discerned (fig. 114).

The years from the inception of the Wiener Werkstätte fashion department to roughly 1914 may be characterized as an experimental phase, during which an attempt was made both to create a distinctive Viennese silhouette and to assimilate foreign influences. In addition to the precedent of the Empire waist, there was also a taste for Oriental touches, which turned up in the theater costumes of Leon Bakst (exhibited at the Cassirer Gallery in Berlin in 1913) and also in the work of Poiret. The principal Viennese residue of this trend was a fascination with "harem" pants or pantaloons, which the Wiener Werkstätte combined rather awkwardly with long jackets and overskirts (fig. 116). Though ungainly and peculiar as streetwear, the harem pants survived into the 1920s as one of the fashion department's most successful items: the silk pajama, which, in keeping with the Werkstätte's domestic thrust, was perfect for lounging about at home (fig. 117). The early designs, however, drew sharp criticism for their impracticality; the Wiener Werkstätte was chided for creating "artist's clothes" that bore no relationship to everyday existence. This problem was in no way ameliorated by the fact that many of the designers really were artists (or, like Wimmer, architects) who probably had no idea how to translate their pretty sketches into wearable garments. Severe problems of execution are revealed by a comparison of some of these early drawings with the finished clothing (figs. 113 and 114).

The temptation to measure the Wiener Werkstätte's fashion achievements against those of the French was unavoidable. To steal the lead in international fashion from the well-established Paris couturiers would have been an unrealistic goal for such a young enterprise, but to at least supplant French design in Austria was a hope whose little flame was fanned by the patriotism of World War I. Already in 1913 the Viennese press began to take a smug pride in the native product. Poiret's models, they sneered, were "all a little on the sassy or flirtatious side"; the Wiener Werkstätte, on the other hand, provided "clothing for decent women."[6] With the war, France became the declared enemy, and the fashion department (like the rest of the Wiener Werkstätte) retreated into a more consciously Austrian aesthetic. There was, for example, something called the "*Alt Wien*" (old Vienna) style, a regurgitation of the 1870s and 1880s, and then there was always good old Biedermeier. While Bertha Zuckerkandl criticized this nineteenth-century revival as a violation of everything the Wiener Werkstätte stood for, it probably helped pull the fanciful "artist's" designs back to a reality that was more readily interpreted by traditionally trained tailors. This, together with accumulating practical experience, resulted in some of the Wiener Werkstätte's first truly suc-

116

117

cessful garments: practical, low-key clothing that reflected the somber tone of the early war years. As the war dragged on, and defeat became more imminent, the fashion industry was swept by the same trend toward escapist, decorative styles that was seen in other branches of the applied arts. Historicist and also "folkish" clothing came to the fore once again, as did a self-conscious use of luxurious materials. Ironically, silk was more easily come by than wool during these years, and it was cunningly draped in tight pleats to reduce the quantity required.

By the end of the war, the Wiener Werkstätte fashion department was a well-established and respected institution. It had achieved its first major international success when the German Crown Princess Cecily patronized a Berlin exhibition at the Hohenzollern Kunstgewerbehaus (Hohenzollern Arts and Crafts House) in 1912, and Werkstätte fashions were prominently displayed at the Cologne Werkbund exhibition in 1914 (fig. 118). During the war, fashion shows were largely limited to domestic efforts such as a large installation designed by Dagobert Peche at the Österreichisches Museum

für Kunst und Industrie in 1915/16 (fig. 119). However, the push toward reestablishing normal international relations grew stronger as the war drew to a close, and fashion presentations were organized in Amsterdam in 1917, and in Zürich and Stockholm in 1918. The short-lived New York branch of the Wiener Werkstätte brought its fashions to the New World in the early 1920s, and continuing cooperation with leading stage personalities at home further enhanced its prestige. In the later 1920s it became common for actresses to double as fashion models, giving their imprimatur to the entire line.

In 1922 Eduard Wimmer, possibly due to the Wiener Werkstätte's growing financial difficulties and differences with Hoffmann, left for the United States. Until 1925, when he returned to Austria, he lived in New York and Chicago, where he taught at the Art Institute. Max Snischek, who had studied textile design at the Kunstgewerbeschule and been a regular contributor to the fashion department at least since the 1914 Werkbund exhibition, apparently took over Wimmer's position. He and Maria Likarz (fig. 151), a former Hoffmann student, now assumed primary responsibility for

118

119

118. Eduard Josef Wimmer-Wisgrill. Wiener Werkstätte room at the Deutscher Werkbund exhibition, Cologne. 1914.

116. Lotte Calm. Wiener Werkstätte-style "harem" ensemble. 1914–15. Hand-colored linoleum print. Signed, lower margin. Published in *Mode Wien*.

117. Wiener Werkstätte pajama. 1920. Silk designed by Dagobert Peche.

119. Dagobert Peche. Fashion exhibition at the Österreichisches Museum für Kunst und Industrie, Vienna. 1915.

120

121

120. Mela Köhler. Fashion
design. Color lithograph postcard (No. 323). 5½″ × 3½″.
Published by the Wiener
Werkstätte.

121. Dagobert Peche. Design
for a dress. 1914. Hand-
colored woodcut. Published
in *Mode Wien.*

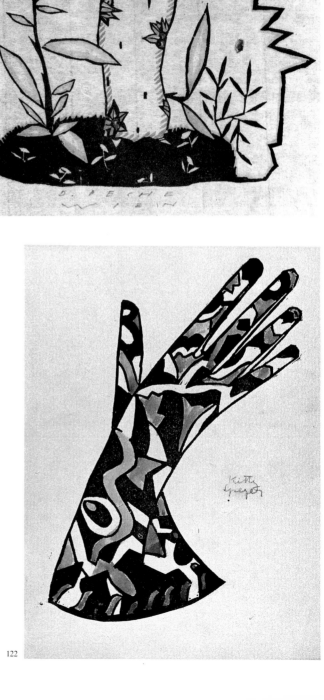

122. Agnes ("Kitty") Speyer.
Design for a glove. Hand-colored linoleum print on laid
paper. Signed, center right.
12¼″ × 9½″. Published in
*Mode Blätter aus der Schule
Hoffmann.*

122

the Werkstätte fashion line; when Snischek left in 1932 to take a teaching post in Munich, Likarz carried on alone for the few remaining months of the Wiener Werkstätte's existence. It is often said that the fashion and textile divisions were the mainstay of the Werkstätte during its declining years, and this statement is to some extent borne out by the fashion department's record of growth: it acquired its own factory-size premises on the Johannesgasse in 1914, and its lavish showroom in the Palais Esterhazy on the Kärntnerstrasse was expanded in 1919/20. Boasting (at least on paper) 150 employees in 1924, it was reconstituted as an independent entity, Modehaus der Wiener Werkstätte Primavesi & Co. (Wiener Werkstätte Fashion House, Primvaesi and Co.). It was reabsorbed into the main enterprise in 1927 as part of the general financial restructuring of that period. The fashion division, as previously noted, was the last branch of the Werkstätte to close in 1932. Nevertheless, it is clear that this division lost considerable steam with Wimmer's departure. Press coverage of its collections dropped off markedly, and for its last years it seems to have made little effort to introduce new lines.

FASHION DEPARTMENT GRAPHICS

If one of the early problems of the Wiener Werkstätte fashion division was the three-dimensional interpretation of sketches by artists who had no training in the construction of garments, it later became necessary to retranslate the actual garments back into two-dimensional representations. Fashion photography as we know it was comparatively late in coming to Vienna, and really only became common in the 1920s. The ungainly poses and unflattering lighting of many of the Werkstätte fashion photos suggest that these were intended only for internal record-keeping (fig. 115). Graphic design was more commonly used to present the "line" to the public. Heddi Hirsch, Mela Köhler, Otto Lendecke, Fritzi Löw and Arnold Nechansky are among the artists who were active as draftsmen for the fashion department, and little watercolor sketches were often sent, together with fabric swatches, to mail-order customers. However, the published drawings of the fashion division, with the exception of the postcards drawn by Köhler to introduce the first collection in 1911 (pl. 32, fig. 114), correspond only vaguely to the actual clothing (fig. 120). At best they evoke the mood or general effect of the style. They could be used to promote the Wiener Werkstätte "feeling," but not to properly order garments.

Of particular interest in this regard are two collections of fashion prints, Mode Wien (Viennese Fashion) and Das Leben einer Dame (The Life of a Lady), published in 1914/15 and 1916 respectively. Although these portfolios were not published by the Wiener Werkstätte (at least its imprint cannot be found on them), all of the participating artists were Kunstgewerbeschule students or graduates, and almost all of them worked for the Wiener Werkstätte at one time or another. The style and technique of the prints are very similar to that of the Mode Blätter (fashion sheets) that Hoffmann's students regularly created (fig. 122). Mode Wien (fig. 121)

consisted of twelve portfolios, each containing twelve prints (mostly hand-colored linoleum cuts, but also woodcuts, etchings and lithographs); Das Leben einer Dame contained twenty prints by many of the same artists (pl. 33). Both publications were limited editions. The first portfolio of Mode Wien was printed in a hundred examples, the remaining eleven only in fifty—ostensibly intended not for distribution to the general public, but for tailor shops. However, as models for specific garments, the prints were virtually useless, perhaps because only a few of the twenty-five artists were actual fashion designers. The portfolios summarize all the prevailing fashion trends—the Empire style, the harem pants, the Biedermeier revival—without precisely documenting them.

As a collaborative venture merging fashion and fine art, the various fashion prints may be considered yet another expression of the Gesamtkunstwerk, albeit in a slightly decadent incarnation. For these prints function neither as practical templates nor as profound artistic statements. Reviewers at the time saw a relationship between the linocuts and German Expressionist woodcuts. Interestingly, printmaking, which was so central to the expressionist aesthetic in Germany, had almost no impact on Austrian fine art. Two of the major artists of this period—Klimt and Gerstl—made no prints whatsoever, and the others—Kokoschka, Kubin, and Schiele—were interested mainly in the essentially reproductive technique of transfer lithography. Whereas the Germans had explored the unique aesthetic capabilities of each printmaking form and elevated the genre to the stature of high art, in Austria printmaking remained largely confined to the realm of Kleinkunst. The preponderance of linocuts among the fashion prints is telling, for this technique retains the graphic flavor of woodcut but lacks the subtleties made possible by wood's grain and texture. The foreign Expressionists had achieved some of their most powerful statements through the medium of woodcut; the Austrians picked up the superficial style and used it for fashion plates.

JEWELRY AND ACCESSORIES

Hoffmann and Moser had begun designing jewelry early on, and this was one of the areas singled out in the 1905 work program. Over the years, additional fashion accessories such as hats (fig. 112), hatpins (fig. 128) and fans (fig. 123) were added. Especially noteworthy are the gilded leather handbags and purses that Hoffmann and others in the leather shop created (fig. 124). The efflorescence of the fashion department naturally encouraged other items to be added to the line: beaded bags, chains and belts (fig. 155), shoe buckles, shoes, umbrellas and shawls. The Artists' Workshops contributed a great deal to the production of these accessories, which were also manufactured by a form of cottage industry; a lady in the Vienna suburb of Mödling specialized in little fabric rosettes.

The work program clearly set out the Wiener Werkstätte's basic philosophy of jewelry design, which eschewed the use of precious stones but not (at least in these rich, early days)

123

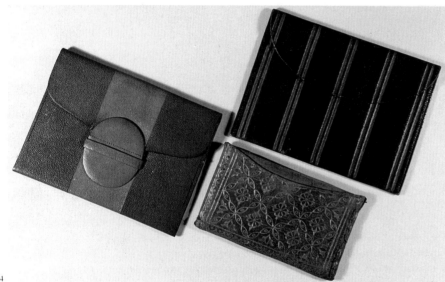

124

123. Berthold Löffler. Fan designed for the Cabaret Fledermaus. Ca. 1904–05. Colored paper and cardboard. 8¼″ × 15⅛″.

124. Josef Hoffmann (*left*), unidentified artist (*upper right*) and Dagobert Peche (*lower right*). Three leather purses. 5¾″ × 4¼″, 5¾″ × 4¼″, and 4¾″ × 2¾″.

125. Women's shoes. Ca. 1914. Colored silk and leather. Executed by the Wiener Werkstätte.

126. Josef Hoffmann. Comb. Ca. 1908. Tortoiseshell and gold.

127. Koloman Moser. Necklace. Ca. 1904–05. Gold and opals.

128. Koloman Moser. Hatpins. Ca. 1905. Gold, opals and semiprecious stones.

129. Koloman Moser. Jewelry design. Ca. 1905. Tempera and ink.

130. Koloman Moser. Jewelry design. Ca. 1905. Tempera and pencil.

125

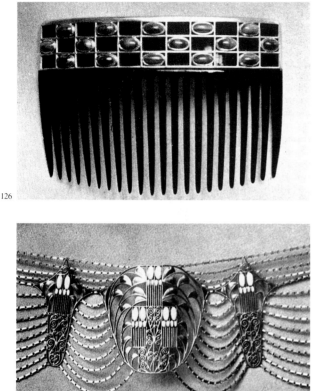

126

128

127

129

precious metals. "We use many semiprecious stones," the tract noted; "they make up in beauty of color and infinite variety what they lack in intrinsic value by comparison with diamonds. We love silver for its sheen and gold for its glitter. In artistic terms, copper is just as valuable as an object made of gold and precious stones."[7] The use of less costly materials also encouraged experimentation, especially on the part of inexperienced Kunstgewerbeschule students. Furthermore, semiprecious stones left more leeway for flights of fancy than did precious stones, which in the style of the day required austere, simple settings. Wiener Werkstätte jewelry designs followed the general stylistic trends of the times. Entering the field in the waning days of Art Nouveau, Hoffmann and Moser, while not entirely rejecting floral motifs, put the brake on Art Nouveau exuberance and introduced a more restrained geometric inventiveness (pl. 39). However, the element of fantasy and decoration is an inherent component of jewelry design, and perhaps for this reason Werkstätte jewelry never felt the full brunt of the purist phase. Jewelry design, furthermore, was one of the first areas in which the new decorative trend, introduced by Czeschka and others around 1905, surfaced. During the war, material shortages shifted the emphasis to works in ivory (fig. 154), and at the express request of Peche an ivory workshop under the direction of Friedrich Nerold was added in 1916. The Artists' Workshops also produced wood and enameled costume jewelry.

130

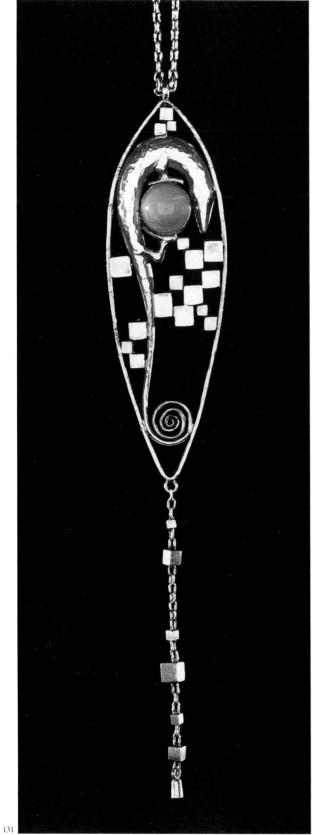

132

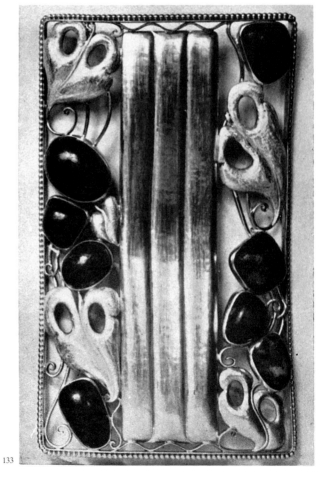

131

133

131. Koloman Moser. Pen-
dant. 1903. Silver and opals.
15¾″ long. Executed by the
Wiener Werkstätte.

132. Eduard Josef Wimmer-
Wisgrill. Pendant. Ca. 1910.
Gold and semiprecious
stones.

133. Eduard Josef Wimmer-
Wisgrill. Belt buckle. Ca.
1910. Silver and turquoise.

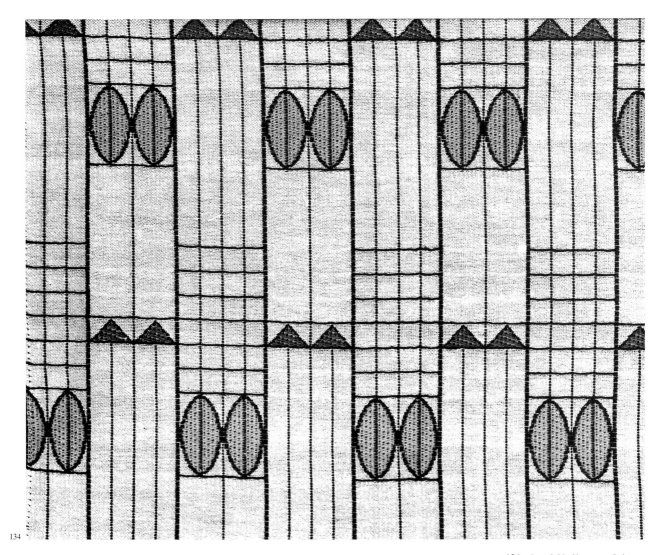

134

TEXTILES

Textiles had been a requisite of modern interior design even before Hoffmann and Moser founded the Wiener Werkstätte, but the introduction of the fashion department saw a turn to the production of fabrics suited to dressmaking—in particular, the hand-printed silks that became a Wiener Werkstätte specialty. The firm of Backhausen began manufacturing carpets (fig. 137) and upholstery fabrics (figs. 134 and 136) after designs by Moser and Hoffmann between 1898 and 1900, and it was among the licensees for the Werkstätte's earliest fabric designs. While it is said that the Werkstätte first began printing its own fabrics in 1905,[8] it appears that a full-fledged textile division was not founded until 1909 or 1910.[9] The timing of the Wiener Werkstätte's entry into textile design suggests a direct connection with the founding of the fashion division, but surprisingly, Werkstätte fabrics were rarely used for the fashions until the late 1920s. There is also, understandably, some question as to which garments were actually designed by the Werkstätte and which used only its fabrics.

The massive output of the Wiener Werkstätte textile department (some eighteen thousand designs by over eighty artists) reflects not only its success, but also its relative accessiblity to artists. Requiring none of the specialized training of fashion design or architecture, it provided an outlet for anyone with graphic talent and was a common meeting ground for artists as diverse as Czeschka, Mathilde Flögl, Hoffmann, Maria Likarz, Berthold Löffler, Moser, Peche and Max Snischek. Students at the Kunstgewerbeschule and members of the Artists' Workshops were also kept busy doing fabric patterns. The most obvious use for all this fabric was clothing, but the activities of the textile division also encouraged the creation of related objects, such as tablecloths and napkins (fig. 142), lampshades and cushions. An important sideline was lacemaking and tulle embroidery (fig. 141). Peche had a particular flair for lacework fantasies, which like his work in other media are really tiny artworks unto themselves—so delicate and precious that one can hardly imagine putting them to any practical use.

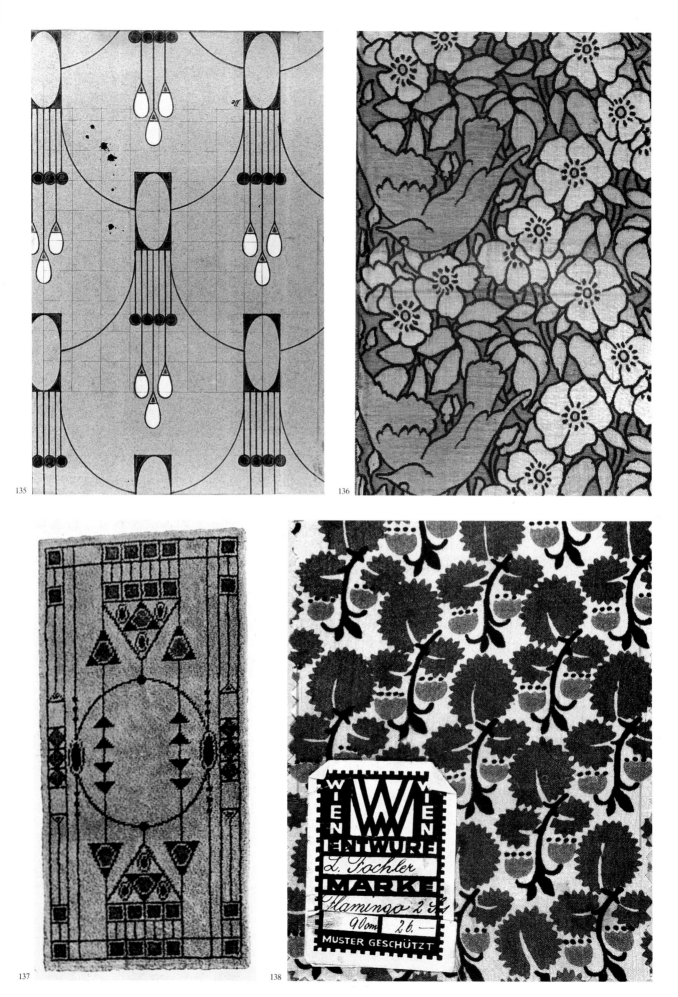

135

136

137

138

135. Otto Prutscher. *Chantilly*. Sketch for a fabric pattern. Executed by Joh. Backhausen & Söhne.

136. Koloman Moser. *Wildrosen* (Wild Roses). 1899. Fabric. Executed by Joh. Backhausen & Söhne.

137. Otto Prutscher. Handknotted carpet. Ca. 1905. Executed by Joh. Backhausen & Söhne.

138. Lotte Föchler-Frömmel. *Flamingo*. Three-colored silk dress fabric. Executed in two different color combinations by the Wiener Werkstätte; one of the earliest Werkstätte fabrics.

139. Josef Hoffmann. *Kohleule* (Night Owl). Three-colored silkscreened silk fabric (No. 366). Executed by the Wiener Werkstätte.

140. *Medea*. Multicolored silk dress fabric (No. 60348). Executed by the Wiener Werkstätte.

139

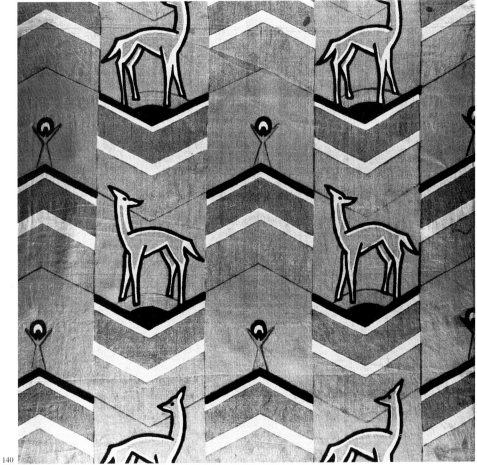

140

141. Dagobert Peche. Two doilies. Ca. 1918–20. Embroidered white bone lace. Each 11⅜″ × 9½″ (oval). Executed by the Wiener Werkstätte.

141

WALLPAPER

Wallpaper design was a natural outgrowth of fabric design, for it required a similarly repetitive application of a two-dimensional pattern. Fabrics themselves had in fact been used as wall coverings in early Wiener Werkstätte interiors, and all of the artists who contributed to the wallpaper collections also designed fabrics. Though wallpaper design was part and parcel of the British Arts and Crafts revival, it was slow in being taken up by the Austrians, who considered paper wall coverings lower class. In addition to fabric, early Wiener Werkstätte walls were decorated with frescoes, paneling and ceramic tiles. All of this changed, however, in 1913, when the Österreichisches Museum für Kunst und Industrie, in cooperation with the native wallpaper industry, invited artists to contribute wallpaper designs to a special exhibition. Ludwig Heinrich Jungickel, Arnold Nechansky and Franz Zülow were among the Wiener Werkstätte artists who licensed their designs to the firm of P. Piette. No fewer than three firms—

Piette, Julius Jaksch, and Thaussig & Co.—showed wallpaper by Peche at the exhibition, and in 1919 Max Schmidt issued the first Peche wallpaper collection (fig. 146). In the early 1920s Philipp Häusler arranged for the Cologne company of Flammersheim und Steinmann to bring out wallpaper collections after designs by Peche and Maria Likarz, and in 1929 Salubra (which had a preexisting relationship with Hoffmann) brought out what was perhaps the most successful collection, after designs by Mathilde Flögl (pl. 34, fig. 145).

Wallpaper had a natural bearing on the development of the *Gesamtkunstwerk* as it related to interior design. Photographs in the large sample books that salesmen brought to the customers' homes suggested how the various patterns might be incorporated in a total design scheme (figs. 143 and 144). Certainly this was a more convenient (and less expensive) way to achieve the Wiener Werkstätte "look" than having Hoffmann personally come over to create a *Gesamtkunstwerk*. Hoffmann saw the wallpaper designs

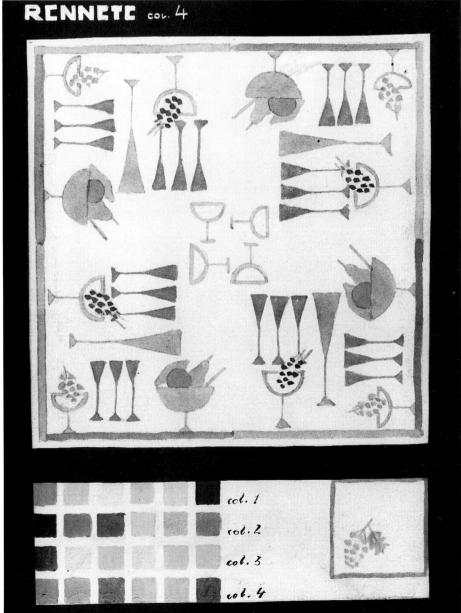

142. Maria Likarz. Sketch for a tablecloth and matching napkins, showing various color combinations. Watercolor on paper. 5¾″ × 5¾″ (image). Sold in the United States by Marshall Field & Co..

142

143

143. Josef Hoffmann. Suggested room setting for a wallpaper designed by Mathilde Flögl and executed by Salubra. 1928.

144. Josef Hoffmann. Suggested room setting for a wallpaper designed by Mathilde Flögl and executed by Salubra. 1928.

144

145. Mathilde Flögl. Wallpaper pattern. 1928. Executed in a variety of color combinations by Salubra.

146. Dagobert Peche. *Semiramis.* 1919. Wallpaper pattern. Executed by Max Schmidt.

145

chiefly as a tool for architects, providing them with a pallette from which to choose in setting the tone of a given room: "simplicity and seriousness, cheerfulness, or indeed solemnity."[10] A more realistic observer, however, likened the wallpaper designs to decorative garments for the home, saying, "A woman will choose them as she chooses the material for a dress or a parasol."[11] The wallpaper patterns, with their variations in color schemes and vast selection of motifs, provided plenty of room for both the professional and the dilettante. Depending on one's abilities, the wallpaper could be incorporated in a serious design program or used merely as decorative frippery. Incompetence in installation was yet another problem, for the geometric designs proved almost impossible to install correctly, as no wall is ideally perpendicular, no floor exactly straight.[12] As the Wiener Werkstätte relinquished its role as architectural overseer and placed its creations in the hands of the less exacting public, the original conception of the *Gesamtkunstwerk* became watered down, diminished by its own success.

146

147

148

149

149. Dagobert Peche. Poster
for the Wiener Werkstätte
fashion division. Color
lithograph.

ARTISTIC CHANGE AND DECLINE

The departure of Koloman Moser in 1907 was a turning
point in the history of the Wiener Werkstätte's aesthetic
development. The quest for geometric simplicity, which had
been pioneered jointly by Moser and Hoffmann, was by this
time already fading. New artists, such as Carl Otto Czeschka
and Berthold Löffler, had introduced an ornamental revival
to the Werkstätte, diluting the strength of the original partners; it was no longer a two-man show. Hoffmann was a collaborative personality who fed off the work of his colleagues
at the Werkstätte and at the Kunstgewerbeschule. He had
originally been influenced by Moser, and he remained open
to equivalent influences at the Werkstätte after Moser left.

147. Dagobert Peche. "Fan-
tasy Pieces." Ca. 1921–22.
Painted tin. Executed by the
Wiener Werkstätte.

148. Dagobert Peche.

150

150. Dagobert Peche. Box in
the shape of an apple. Ca. 1918–20.
Silver. 7″ high. Executed by the
Wiener Werkstätte.

Eduard Wimmer-Wisgrill, who had studied with Hoff-mann at the Kunstgewerbeschule, was the first major person-ality to join the Wiener Werkstätte after Moser's resignation, but his influence as director of the fashion department was nothing compared to that of the flamboyant Dagobert Peche, who was appointed manager of the Artists' Workshops in 1915 (fig. 148). Peche had met Hoffmann at a banquet in honor of Otto Wagner in 1911, the same year that he gradua-ted from Vienna's Academy of Fine Art, and from the start, it seems, he dazzled everyone with his inventive facility. "We felt that each of his drawings was something valuable, inspired and wonderful," Hoffmann recalled, "and we always waited impatiently for him to come up with new ideas."[13] Peche's vision was a near antithesis to the practical down-to-earth concerns that had heretofore dominated the Wiener Werkstätte. Of a slightly mystical bent, Peche believed that "art is the attempt to perceive the invisible rhythm that sur-rounds us in order to discover its laws and bring order to chaos."[14] Yet there is somehow more chaos than order to his designs, as though the nice, plain objects of the early Wiener Werkstätte had been left to sit in a jungle for ten years and then been returned, overgrown with wild vines and exotic fruits (fig. 150). Peche proved a fitting replacement for the "man of a thousand talents,"[15] Koloman Moser, for he was equally willing to forge into almost every area of design, from the graphic (fig. 149) to the plastic arts (fig. 147). To the Wie-ner Werkstätte's interiors he added a new element of theatri-cality; his installation for the 1915 fashion show was actually framed by floor-to-ceiling curtains (fig. 119). In 1917, after fulfilling his obligations to the Austrian army, Peche was sent to open the Werkstätte's Zürich branch (fig. 28). He came back to Vienna in 1919 already suffering from the illness that

151. Maria Likarz.

152. Vally Wieselthier.

was to claim his life and embarked on some of his most outrageous experiments in gold and silver, creating bizarre, sometimes nearly abstract sculptures without any apparent regard for either function or cost.

After Peche's death in 1923, Julius Zimpel, who had studied under Moser at the Kunstgewerbeschule, joined Hoffmann as artistic codirector of the Wiener Werkstätte. Zimpel was essentially a graphic designer, calligrapher and bookbinder whose taste for baroque ornament showed definite traces of Peche's influence. His premature death in 1925 left the Wiener Werkstätte again floundering for artistic leadership: Hoffmann himself was intermittently ill throughout the early 1920s, and Wimmer had gone to America in 1922. The men were abandoning ship, and suddenly it seemed that the Werkstätte was staffed almost entirely by women. Arts and crafts had always been a suitable occupation for a "lady," and the draining of the male population during the war swelled the ranks of female Kunstgewerbeschule students. Thus it was that women very naturally entered the Wiener Werkstätte's upper echelons in the 1920s. In the fashion division, Maria Likarz (fig. 151) held down the fort together with Max Snischek. Around 1913, Powolny and Löffler's Wiener Keramik, suffering from financial difficulties, merged with the Gmundner Keramik;[16] the next generation of ceramicists— Gudrun Baudisch, Susi Singer and Vally Wieselthier (fig. 152) foremost among them—was largely female. All of these women, plus others such as Mathilde Flögl, Hilda Jesser, Mela Köhler, Fritzi Löw, and Felice Rix, functioned as illustrators and general "decorators," creating patterns and motifs for a broad range of Werkstätte products and thereby giving their imprint to the entire line.

In the minds of the Wiener Werkstätte's critics—and by the mid-1920s these included a number of people besides the always irascible Adolf Loos—the artistic decline of the Werkstätte product was directly attributable to the female influence. Julius Klinger, a disgruntled artist whose attacks were so venomous they actually occasioned a libel suit, coined a new name, "*Wiener Weiberkunstgewerbe*" (Viennese Vixen's Arts and Crafts), to go with the familiar "WW" logo. While it may be true that some of these women (to quote Loos) were merely "Fräuleins who regard handicrafts as something whereby one may earn pin money or while away one's spare time until one can walk up the aisle,"[17] most of the Werkstätte's leading craftswomen were serious professionals who devoted their entire lives to their careers.[18] Objectively speaking, the predominance of women probably did contribute something to the Werkstätte's turn to more ephemeral objects, for women were not traditionally permitted to enter such "male" domains as architecture and furniture design.[19] However, the shift to a more decorative, stereotypically feminine aesthetic had been introduced not by the women, but by men—initially by Czeschka and Löffler, and later by Peche and Zimpel. It was less a reflection of the particular sexual makeup of the Werkstätte than of the tenor of the times.

Even before World War I, Austria had begun to reinvestigate native and traditional forms. Hoffmann's return to Biedermeier and vernacular precedents, together with the folk

153

154

155

153. Vally Wieselthier. Bowl.
Ca. 1920–25. Glazed painted
ceramic. 3″ high. Executed by
the Wiener Werkstätte.

154. Dagobert Peche. Tiara.
Ca. 1920. Carved ivory and
gold. 2¾″ × 5⅛″. Executed by
the Wiener Werkstätte.

155. Amalie Szeps. Beaded
band and earrings. Ca. 1920.

art fad, developed into a full-blown aggressive provincialism under the pressure of the war and subsequent defeat. Faced with defeat, the Austrian response (unlike that of the Germans) was not to fight, but to retreat. Theirs was a retreat into fantasy and innocence—an attempt to exaggerate rather than to deny their weaknesses, to appear innocuous. This led to a grand flowering of *Kleinkunst*, in which everything became small and cute. Childishness (fostered by the pioneering children's art teacher Franz Cizek), folkishness and femininity were "in"; the bold, innovative forms of the earlier years were "out." The effects of this were seen both in the multiplication of trinkets—toys (figs. 156 and 158), Christmas ornaments and things of that kind—and in stylistic changes wrought upon more traditional items: ceramic dishes with rough, peasanty glazes (fig. 153), or ornate, Biedermeier-style painted glasses (pls. 23 and 24). Not only did the war encourage the retreat into the decorative and charming, it also, by creating shortages of precious materials, led to a reliance on cheaper substances, such as feathers or papier-mâché. The flow of silver and gems ebbed; the use of ceramics, wood and beads increased.

A scene from Joseph Roth's novel about the period between the wars, *The Imperial Tomb (Die Kapuzinergruft)*, sums up the phenomenon succinctly. The hero, having just returned home from the war, asks his mother what has happened to his estranged wife. The mother's eyes suggest some horrible fate, and the son, trying to imagine what might evoke such a reaction, guesses that his wife must have become "a dancer":

My mother shook her head gravely. Then she said sadly, almost mournfully, "No, a craftswoman. Do you know what that is? She designs, or rather carves, in fact—crazy necklaces and rings, modern things, you know, all corners, and clasps of fir. I believe she can also plait straw mats...."

"Is that so bad, then?"

"Worse than that, boy! When people start using worthless material to make something which looks as if it has some value, where will it all stop? ... No one can persuade me that cotton is linen or that you can make a wreath of laurels out of pine needles."[20]

The Wiener Werkstätte had to make do, at least symbolically, with cotton instead of linen, pine needles instead of laurels. Whether this was innocent escapism or (as the mother in Roth's novel suggests) out and out fraud is a matter of opinion. It was, at any rate, an approach that not only implicitly violated the grand ideals of the Werkstätte's early years, but that would have been unthinkable when Austria was still an empire, whole and prosperous. Behind the cheap little trinkets lay a humiliation and a loss so profound that they could only be concealed by such delightful inconsequentialities. As one contemporary commented, "We are as poor as beggars, and go about in rags, but we cloak ourselves in the mantle of beauty and thereby rise above it all."[21]

Austria's aesthetic provincialism effectively cut the nation off from the development of modernism abroad, and may be partially responsible for the failure of the Wiener Werkstätte in Paris in 1925 and in Berlin in 1929. Much prewar Werkstätte design, with its streamlined shapes and zigzag patterns, actually anticipated Art Deco, but its postwar style was popular only at home. Whereas its spiritual ancestor, the Seces-

156

157

158

156. Dagobert Peche. Toy
animals. Ca. 1921–22. Silk and
beads. Executed by the Wiener Werkstätte.

157. Mela Köhler. Illustration from *Klein Friedels Tag*
(Little Friedel's Day). Ca.
1920. Children's book. Published by Konegens
Jugendschriften-verlag.

158. Josef Hoffmann. Toy
factory. Ca. 1920. Painted
wooden building blocks.
Approximately ¼″ to 5″ high.

sion, had fought to bring Austria into contact with developments abroad, the Werkstätte now rejected the leading foreign innovations, including (or especially) the Bauhaus. What had once been a progressive movement became almost wholly reactionary. The Wiener Werkstätte, whose earliest experiments had bordered on pure abstraction, now vociferously denounced this trend. As abstraction became more firmly established throughout Western Europe, Austrian art remained resolutely figurative, endlessly repeating the formulae of the earlier Expressionist generation, or spinning off the German *Neue Sachlichkeit* (new realism) style into a typically Austrian variant: "magic" realism.

Another problem that plagued the Wiener Werkstätte during its waning years was the growing influence of Kunstgewerbeschule students and former students. The Kunstgewerbeschule connection, once an asset, now became a liability. The golden opportunity that Hoffmann and others offered their students—to sell their class assignments to the Werkstätte and actually be paid for them while they were still in school—inevitably encouraged a degree of amateurism, for talented though the students might be, they were not yet full-fledged professionals. The ranks of Werkstätte artists were increased dramatically in the process, but the level of quality was not. The standard program of instruction at the Kunstgewerbeschule involved several years of training in a range of subjects, followed by the option of admission to a master class in one of the specialized departments.[22] Although Hoffmann ostensibly taught the master class for architecture, and Moser the class for decorative painting, both classes functioned more like general design seminars. Students, especially in later years, rarely saw the great man Hoffmann, but rather came in every day to sit at large tables and work at whatever project struck their fancy.[23] While the assumption was that one was admitted to a master class (traditionally the final level of an arts education in Austria, also at the Academy) only when one had mastered the rudiments and was therefore ready to work independently, there is some question as to whether this was actually the case at the Kunstgewerbeschule.[24] If Hoffmann was not really teaching architecture, and Moser not painting, what choice (other than the conservative Academy) did students who wanted to learn these disciplines have? The Wiener Werkstätte believed that a painter like Moser could design furniture, or an architect like Wimmer could design clothing; the question was, could they design them well? In its attempt to encourage competence in all branches of design, the Kunstgewerbeschule in fact fostered competence in none, and the original crafts ethic of the Werkstätte was subverted. The truth was that Hoffmann and Moser had themselves been products of the rigorous, specialized academic training that they as teachers now opposed. The Wiener Werkstätte had originally attracted artists with multiple talents; producing them, however, was something else again.

One by one the Wiener Werkstätte's original ideals were falling by the wayside: integrity in the use of materials was less easily achieved in the era of postwar shortages; the retreat into native Austrian forms effectively undermined the innovative thrust of the earlier years; the educational pro-

gram at the Kunstgewerbeschule encouraged the proliferation of dilletante designers rather than enlightened craftsmen. The final and most important ideal that the Wiener Werkstätte sacrificed was that of the *Gesamtkunstwerk* itself. In the postwar climate of diminished expectations and resources, there were few opportunities to execute lavish architectural projects on a prewar scale, and the severing of Hoffmann's architectural practice from the Werkstätte proper further served to weaken the collaborative thrust. Meanwhile, the expansion of retail outlets, industrial licenses, and such items as the wallpaper collections effectively eliminated the architect's supervisory role. From now on the public was free to determine how and where Werkstätte objects would be placed in a room, and whether they would be joined by others of their kind or forced to coexist with tasteless commercial junk. While from a fiscal point of view it may be true that the Werkstätte failed to make enough concessions to the realities of commerce, from a personal point of view the enterprise made enormous efforts to please. As Moser noted after he quit, "In my opinion, the activities were…all too dependent on the taste of the customer. And at the same time, the public usually had no idea what it actually wanted."[25] Hoffmann, who had never had any dogmatic stylistic convictions, was all too easily swayed by such popular fads as folkishness. He and Moser had dreamed of complete artistic control, but without a stylistic program, there was really nothing to control.

With the weakening of the *Gesamtkunstwerk* concept, the Wiener Werkstätte lost its moral force. In many ways this fate was predictable, for the Werkstätte was torn apart by contradictions that had been inherent from the start. As an artist-run business enterprise, the Werkstätte had always been plagued by the conflict between artistic and financial considerations. This cut both ways, weakening the enterprise's financial stability while at the same time eroding the artistic resolve of its directors by subjecting them to the whims of the public. The dual program of crafts and industrial licensing cracked under the pressure of the postwar industrial climate, which prohibited compromise solutions and demanded a choice. The desire to abandon historical precedent, which Hoffmann had once so eagerly professed, came in conflict with his own ingrained traditionalism and the conservative shift of the Austrian nation as a whole: again, a choice had to be made; the dualism would no longer hold up. But the worst and most devastating contradiction was the one that Loos had seen all along: the conflict between decoration and functionalism, between art and artifact. Loos's prophecy—that these diametrically opposed impulses could not remain wedded without the grander purpose of art being debased—proved correct. In the silver fantasies of Dagobert Peche, the ceramic figurines of Vally Wieselthier, and the linocuts of the fashion illustrators, fine art impulses became submerged in *Kleinkunst*. From craftsmanship the Wiener Werkstätte had descended into the *Kunstgewerbliches*—the artsy-craftsy. The result was work that was neither functional nor truly artistic, but that occupied a hazy middle ground. The noble ideals of both art and functionalism had been subverted by the petty and the pretty.

29

29. Koloman Moser. Formal
dress. Ca. 1901–06. 51⅛″ long.

30. Max Snischek. Sketch for a Wiener Werkstätte coat. 1914. Watercolor and pencil on paper. Initialed and dated, lower right.

31. Mela Köhler. Fur-trimmed hat and muff. Color lithograph postcard (No. 177). 5½″ × 3½″. Published by the Wiener Werkstätte.

32. Mela Köhler. Wiener Werkstätte dress. 1911. Color lithograph postcard (No. 519). 5½″ × 3½″. Published by the Wiener Werkstätte.

33. Reni Schaschl. Fashion illustration. 1916. Hand-colored linoleum print. Published in *Das Leben einer Dame*.

31

32

33

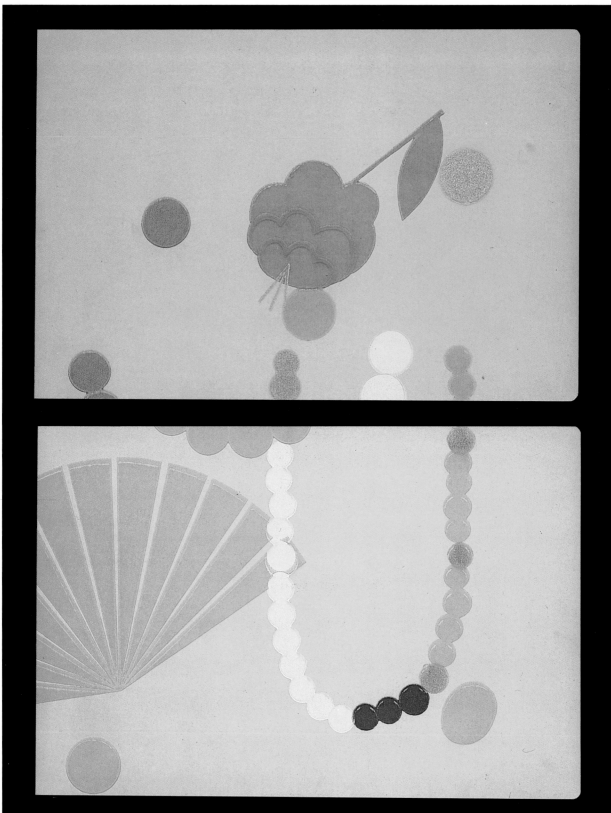

34. Mathilde Flögl. Wallpaper
pattern. 1928. Executed in a
variety of color combinations
by Salubra.

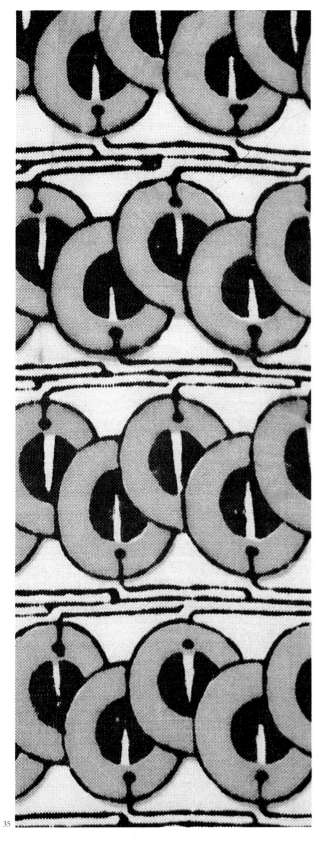

35. Koloman Moser. *Baum-
falke* (Treehawk). Ca. 1905.
Two-colored silkscreened silk
fabric. Executed by the Wiener
Werkstätte; one of the earliest
Werkstätte fabrics.

36. Carl Otto Czeschka. *Wald-
idyll* (Woodland Idyll). Multicolored silk dress fabric (No.
531). Executed by the Wiener
Werkstätte.

37

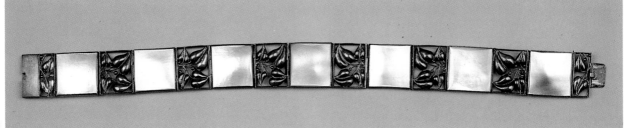

38

37. Four boxes. Ca. 1917–19.
Hand-painted wood and glass.
Executed by the Wiener
Werkstätte.

38. Josef Hoffmann. Neck-
lace. Ca. 1908. Gold plate and
mother-of-pearl.

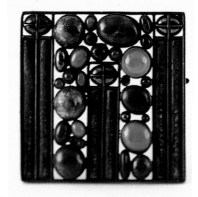

39

40

39. Josef Hoffmann. Brooch.
Ca. 1904–06. Silver and semiprecious stones. Approxi-
mately 2″ × 2″.

40. Unidentified artist (*top*)
and Berthold Löffler (*bottom*).
Enamel pendant and gold but-
ton. Ca. 1920 and ca. 1908.

41

42

41. Vally Wieselthier. Sketch
for a stove flue. Before 1929.
Watercolor on paper.
4⅜″ × 6⅛″ (image).

42. Max Snischek. Decorative
motifs for matchboxes. Ca.
1926–28. Enamel on metal.
16⅛″ × 24″.

43

44

45

46

THE GRAPHIC ARTS AND THE BIRTH OF EXPRESSIONISM

The German artist Max Liebermann once quipped that while there were, indeed, "painters" in Vienna, what they painted was mainly carpets and curtains.[1] Certainly it is true that, with the exception of Gustav Klimt, the Secession produced few painters of major talent; it was the applied artists, the Stylists, who were the leaders. The founding of the Wiener Werkstätte and the subsequent departure of the *Klimtgruppe* from the Secession were not events that seemed likely to change this situation.

The weight of the avant-garde came down firmly on the side of the Werkstätte and its educational arm, the Kunstgewerbeschule. Thus it was, at least initially, that the *fin-de-siècle* artistic renaissance found its most congenial two-dimensional outlet not in the fine, but in the graphic arts. The graphic arts constituted the glue that held the Wiener Werkstätte together. Almost every artist toyed with such basic devices as decorative borders and graphic vignettes (fig. 159), or played with patterns that might turn up on anything from wallpaper to bathrobes. As the Werkstätte began to rely more and more on surface ornamentation, the patterns created by these artists became more and more central to its collective style. The fact that its artists could produce designs that were adaptable to a range of crafts applications is one of the reasons that the Wiener Werkstätte, for all its diversity, was nonetheless able to maintain a relatively coherent stylistic image, and that its various divisions seem, over the years, to follow the same general trends.

43. Berthold Löffler. *Cherub with Bell.* Postcard No. 620.
44. Unidentified artist. Easter greeting. Postcard No. 151.
45. Josef Diveky. *The Werewolf.* 1911. Postcard No. 497.
46. Moritz Jung (attr.). *Schönbrunn: At the Zoo.* Postcard No. 658.

Color lithographs published by the Wiener Werkstätte. Each 5½" × 3½".

159. Josef Bruckmüller. Monogram and end paper designs. Ca. 1903–04. Color lithograph. Published in *Die Fläche.*

160. Josef Hoffmann. Weeping willow ornament. Ink on graph paper. 16⅜" × 11⅝".

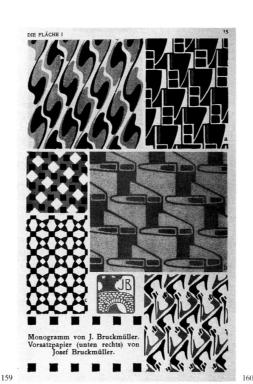

DIE FLÄCHE I   15

Monogramm von J. Bruckmüller.
Vorsatzpapier (unten rechts) von
Josef Bruckmüller.

159

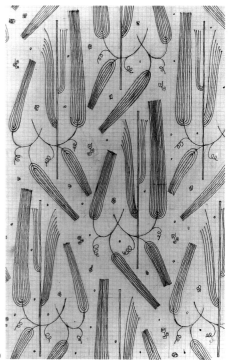

160

TYPOGRAPHY AND BOOK DESIGN

In the graphic arts, as in all other branches of the arts, the wave of change that swept over Austria at the turn of the century originated abroad, in the Art Nouveau of France and the *Jugendstil* of Germany. The improved communications of the later nineteenth century, and in particular the perfection of printing methods that facilitated the juxtaposition of type and illustrations, ushered in a new era of art journals. Periodicals such as the *Revue Blanche* (started in 1891) in France, *The Studio* (1893) in England, and *Pan* (1895), *Simplicissimus* (1896), and *Jugend* (1896) in Germany were international in their scope and impact. Each of these publications was as different in style as it was in content and intent. *The Studio* was a serious arts and design review that published illustrated essays, while *Simplicissimus*, a satirical journal, pioneered a cartoonlike melding of art and captions. *Jugend* was a general-circulation magazine that aimed to please its

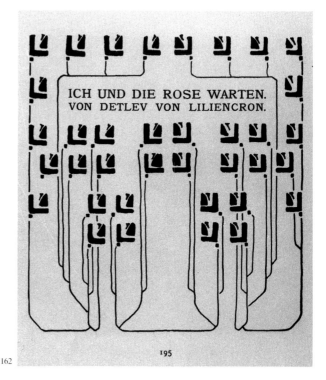

161. Josef Hoffmann (border) and Koloman Moser (initial letter). Page from *Ver Sacrum*. 1898.

162. Josef Bruckmüller. Design for a title page. Ca. 1902. Published in *Ver Sacrum*.

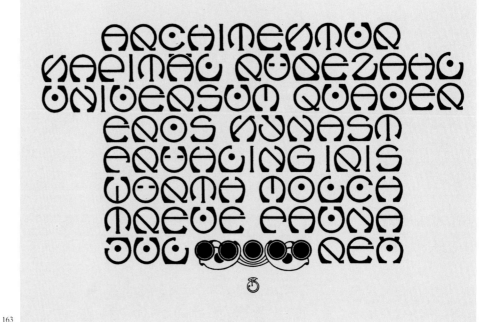

163. Adalb Carl Fischl. Typographical design. Ca. 1900. Published in *Beispiele künstlerischer Schrift.*

large audience with its jokes and "modern" style (it gave its name to the term *Jugendstil*); *Pan*, with its limited-edition graphics, was directed at connoisseurs.

It is thus understandable that one of the first acts of the Secession was to organize its own journal, *Ver Sacrum* (Sacred Spring), along the lines of the art journals then generally in vogue. It is impossible, however, to cite any of the aforementioned foreign magazines as a specific model for *Ver Sacrum*. Like so many of the Austrian *fin-de-siècle* innovations, it drew on foreign influences but converted them into something entirely unique. *Ver Sacrum* was at the same time a work of art in itself and a commentary upon contemporary art. It contained conventional essays illustrated by halftones, as well as original prints and graphically harmonious spreads (fig. 161). Conceived as a totality, it was yet another variation of the *Gesamtkunstwerk*: a complete little artwork consisting of coordinated typography, design and illustration. *Ver Sacrum* was the first—and perhaps the most original—but by no means the last of the publications that supported the Austrian arts revival. One of the most beautiful of the others was

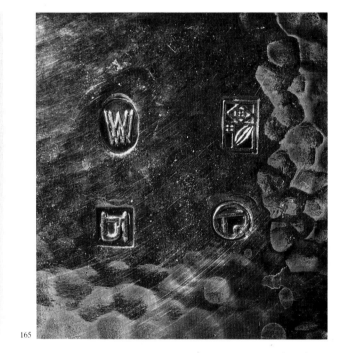

164. Artists' monograms, designed for the Beethoven exhibition. 1902.

165. Silver punches showing the marks of the Wiener Werkstätte and its artist/ craftsmen.

166. Monograms of Wiener Werkstätte artists, as published in the *Kachelalmanach*. 1928.

167. Monograms and trademarks of the Wiener Werkstätte, as published in its 1905 work program.

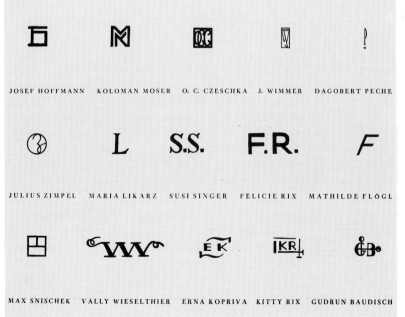

Die Fläche, published by the Anton Schroll Verlag from around 1902 or 1903 (pl. 50). *Die Fläche* (literally, "the surface"), produced in portfolio form, was formulated as a *Musterbuch*, or pattern book, of graphic insignia and poster designs. *Die Fläche*, like *Ver Sacrum*, was conceived as an art object, but there were also more conventional design journals that merely reported about the new art movement. In Germany, Alexander Koch's *Deutsche Kunst und Dekoration* (German Art and Decor), founded in Darmstadt in 1897, published feature articles about the Wiener Werkstätte in almost every issue. At home, Arthur von Scala had beefed up the bulletin of the Österreichisches Museum für Kunst und Industrie and, in 1898, changed its name to *Kunst und Kunsthandwerk* (Art and Handicraft). Other publications had more direct ties with Werkstätte artists, such as the journal *Hohe Warte*, which took its name from Hoffmann's villa colony and was founded by his friend Josef August Lux in 1904, or the short-lived *Damenwelt* (Ladies' World), put out by Otto Lendecke in 1917 as an adjunct to the activites of the fashion department.

The close relationship that existed between the early-twentieth-century arts revival and the publications that brought it to the attention of the public soon led to the evolution of a distinctive typographical style. The so-called Secession type, which was often criticized for being decorative to the point of illegibility (fig. 163), was principally formulated by Rudolf von Larisch, who taught typography and heraldry at the Kunstgewerbeschule. He formulated a theory of positive and negative space, which by giving the same emphasis to both, equalized the pictorial weight of foreground and background. Larisch published his theories in a three-volume study, *Beispiele künstlerischer Schrift* (Examples of Artistic Lettering; 1900, 1903, and 1906), to which Moser, Löffler and Roller, among others, contributed. A great deal of attention was given to creating unique decorative typefaces, initial letters in the Gothic manner, geometric borders, and lettering that emulated handwriting. Combining these custom-made motifs with a limited range of very basic typefaces (fig. 162) was more important than the manipulation of preexisting standard typefaces (which was to become the mainstay of mechanized photocomposition). The characteristic Viennese tendency to use modern technology to approximate the appearance of an archaic craft rather than to create new forms caused its typographical innovations to date quickly. By the time the Wiener Werkstätte published its twenty-fifth anniversary catalogue in 1928 (called the *Kachelalmanach* because its papier-mâché cover resembled a tile), its typographical style seemed hopelessly outmoded.

To the extent that typography could be accommodated to the *Gesamtkunstwerk* concept, the Secessionists and Werkstätte artists tried to ensure that every bit of lettering would bear the conscious imprint of the movement. The Werkstätte went so far as to replace the periods on its office typewriters with little squares, so that even invoices and memos became works of art. The designing of monograms and logos was a particular passion with turn-of-the-century artists, and such insignia often replaced the conventional signature on works of art. The 1903 Beethoven exhibition catalogue contained a glossary of artists' monograms (fig. 164) that can be considered prototypes of the monograms that Wiener Werkstätte artists and craftsmen later affixed to their products. Ideally, every Werkstätte item was to contain four such marks (fig. 165): the "WW" logo itself, the so-called Rosemark, the designer's initials, and the craftsman's initials.[2] The Rosemark, registered in 1903, was the Wiener Werkstätte's first trademark. The actual name "Wiener Werkstätte" was registered only in 1913, and the distinctive double-W logo, probably designed by Moser in the early years, was registered in 1914.[3] The logo was used by itself and also in a square construction together with the spelled-out name of the firm. The monograms that the individual artists and craftsmen used to identify their work (figs. 166 and 167) were published in the 1905 work program and in the *Kachelalmanach*, but in practice the use of these monograms is far less ubiquitous than the Werkstätte originally intended, and even with access to the various published lists, indecipherable marks constantly turn up.

In keeping with the *Gesamtkunstwerk* approach, typography was carefully coordinated with any accompanying illustration, and in fact some of the most distinctive typographical designs of the period can scarcely be distinguished from their decorative surroundings (fig. 64). Larisch's theories about positive and negative space were applied to illustrations as well as to typefaces, and the type, in turn, functioned as an integral part of the overall design rather than occupying the subordinate role of mere caption. The focus of such exercises could be as private as an ex-libris (the Werkstätte designed many of these for its customers) or as public as a poster. However, such single-sheet items were far less interesting, from the *Gesamtkunstwerk* point of view, than books or periodicals. *Ver Sacrum*, after Moser's departure in 1902, ceased to function as a proper *Gesamtkunstwerk* and gradually suspended publication; the later design journals fulfilled a more strictly reportorial function. Thus the Wiener Werkstätte's philosophy of book-as-art-object lent itself principally to two applications: the children's book and the artist's book. Its best-known publication, Oskar Kokoschka's adult fairy tale *Die träumenden Knaben* (The Dreaming Boys), was both (fig. 190). Children's stories, which to this day dominate the genre of the illustrated book, were particularly suited to the Werkstätte's later period, with its interest in the childlike and folkish, and many of the later artists, among them Berthold Löffler and Fritzi Löw excelled at this form. The artist's book, too, benefited strangely from the postwar economic climate. As often happens in inflationary times, the notion of art as investment, heretofore alien to the Austrian ideal of cultural largesse, encouraged the acquisition of various tangible assets. Publishers of deluxe, limited-edition art books such as the Verlag Neuer Graphik (New Graphics Press) proliferated during the hyperinflation of the early 1920s. Housed within the exquisite bindings and slipcases of the resulting publications, whose contributors included Ludwig Heinrich Jungnickel and Julius Zimpel, were specially commissioned illustrations, customized calligraphy and sometimes also limited-edition original prints, signed and numbered by the artist.

The Wiener Werkstätte took the same pains in producing books and other items that it did in designing them. "Have we perhaps forgotten that the love with which a book has

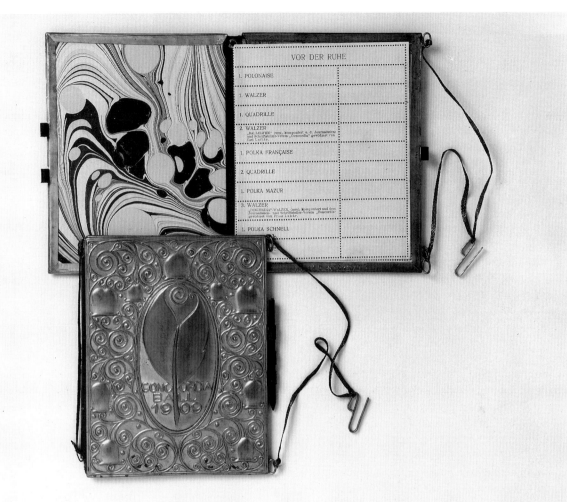

168

169

168. Josef Hoffmann. Program for the Concordia Ball. 1909. Gold-plated brass covers with leather spine and clasp. 5⅝″ × 4½″.

169. Josef Hoffmann. Book cover. Ca. 1921. Gold tooled leather. 8½″ × 6″. Executed by the Wiener Werkstätte.

170. Koloman Moser. Book cover for *Das ewige Licht* (The Eternal Light) by Peter Rosegger. Ca. 1909. 8″ × 5½″.

170

171.

171. Koloman Moser. Cover
for *Ver Sacrum*. 1899.

172. Koloman Moser. *Trout
Cycle*. 1899. Design for a fabric. Published in *Ver Sacrum*.

173. Hilde Exner. Design for
a stenciled poster. Ca. 1903–
04. Color lithograph. Published in *Die Fläche*.

172.

DIE FLÄCHE I   74

Entwurf für ein schabloniertes Plakat von Hilde Exner.
Auf Seite 72 zwei Entwürfe für schablonierte Geschäftskarten
☐ von Emma Schlangenhausen und Josef Bruckmüller. ☐

173.

been printed, decorated and bound creates a completely different relationship between it and us, and that intercourse
with beautiful things makes us beautiful?" the 1905 work program asked rhetorically. "A book must be a work of art in
itself, and its value must be assessed as such."[4] The Werkstätte had its own letterpress shop and sometimes acted as its
own publisher, but it also farmed out projects to independent
publishers and used many of the excellent printers with which
Vienna was endowed. The process of photographically separating illustrations into four standardized component colors
had not yet been altogether perfected and did not have the
pervasive influence that it does today. Especially when repro-

ducing art, it was still customáry to match the artist's exact
colors individually, a practice that gives far brighter, clearer
results than can be achieved photomechanically. The printers
with whom the Wiener Werkstätte worked—among them
Albert Berger and Brüder Rosenbaum—were still craftsmen,
and the brilliance of early-twentieth-century Viennese graphics is owed partly to their skill.

   In tandem with printing, the Wiener Werkstätte was
almost inordinately interested in quality bookbinding (figs.
168, 169 and 170). The 1905 work program devoted two
rather long paragraphs to the subject, and the Werkstätte's
first little exhibition, held that same year at the Galerie

174

175

176

174. Josef Hoffmann. Sculpted wall relief designed for the Beethoven exhibition. 1902.

175. Koloman Moser. Stained-glass window designed for the Beethoven exhibition. 1902.

176. Eduard Josef Wimmer-Wisgrill. "Stoclet Dress," designed for the Wiener Werkstätte. 1911. Wimmer based the embroidered motif on Klimt's frieze.

Miethke, in fact concentrated exclusively on decorative bindings. The revival of bookbinding had been an important component of the British Arts and Crafts movement, but here, as in so many other ideas that they cribbed from Morris and Ruskin, the Werkstätte ideologues exaggerated the impending threat of mass production. When the Werkstätte opened its leather shop (among its first priorities), Hoffmann and Moser found that they had a long and still thriving tradition of native craftsmanship to draw upon. An unknown man, Karl Beitel, presented himself at their door and volunteered to close down his own business so as to put himself at their exclusive service. Exacting craftsmanship was complemented

by exquisite materials—hand-tooled leather, real gold embossing and beautifully marbled and printed end papers—to achieve the look and feel of the book as artwork. This sort of elegance was well suited to special projects such as the Staatsdruckerei Jubilee in 1904 or to the private libraries of the Werkstätte's wealthy clients. However, it was impossible to make such work available on a wider basis, and therefore the Werkstätte's most elaborate books were done only on commission.

GRAPHIC STYLE

The Wiener Werkstätte's distinctive graphic style, with antecedents dating back to the early days of the Secession, eventually found a number of outlets, including posters, advertisements, postcards, broadsheets, and various illustrations for stories, poems, articles and the like. In the largest sense, graphic design was part of everything the Werkstätte did, from decorated glassware to special event-oriented items such as the programs created for the Cabaret Fledermaus (fig. 177). Because graphic design was pervasive, it reflected the comprehensive stylistic development of the period, from the fading Art Nouveau of the late 1890s to the decadence of the postwar period, with its self-conscious naïveté and folkish touches. However, graphics also provided an arena in which fine and applied art met, and therefore graphic design reveals certain impulses that are slightly different from those found in the bulk of the Wiener Werkstätte's output. Graphic design touched the fine arts in three particular areas, each corresponding to a movement in painting: Symbolism (during the early, Art Nouveau phase), Abstraction (during the purist phase) and Expressionism (during the decorative phase).

Association with graphic artists such as Moser, as well as the influence of the foreign Symbolist paintings shown at the Secession, undoubtedly helped Klimt break out of the historicist mold that had shaped his work during the 1880s and early 1890s, when he was considered Makart's logical successor. Klimt's poster for the Secession's first exhibition established a formally ingenious tension between the vacant central expanse and the surrounding type and imagery (fig. 1). More important than its layout, however, was the poster's graphic treatment of a fairly conventional allegorical subject of the sort typically found in academic painting of the period. This graphic treatment endowed the figures with a symbolic significance that transcended the particular mythological reference (Theseus slaying the Minotaur) to give it a contemporary connotation (art triumphs over Philistinism). What had been

implicit in much history painting (that we are to identify with the kings and gods of ages past) became explicit (these kings and gods are here today) when the trappings of a wholly realistic presentation were abandoned. A graphic approach made it possible to relinquish the more earthbound formulations of the Symbolists (as seen in the fully three-dimensional figures that populate Fernand Khnopff's or Ferdinand Hodler's paintings, or Klimt's university allegories [fig. 25]) in favor of a more stylized interpretation (as seen in the work of Toorop, or Klimt's Beethoven and Stoclet friezes [pls. 2 and 3]). The rejection of realistic verisimilitude left Klimt open to two aesthetic impulses—abstraction and decoration—that were to have important ramifications in the applied arts.

Klimt's characteristic *femme fatale*, with her flowing tresses and sublimated eroticism (pl. 47), has her counterpart in the sensuous curves and twirling tendrels of conventional Art Nouveau. Moser, who had supported himself as a professional illustrator for a number of years before the founding of the Secession, was intimately familiar with Art Nouveau and German *Jugendstil* graphic formulations. He, too, had a predilection for images of seductive, long-haired women (fig. 171), but his *fin-de-siècle* posters also presage the impending era of graphic simplification (pl. 48). Japanese prints, which were collected by a number of Secessionist artists, led the way in Austria, just as they had in France a generation earlier, to the treatment of figures as flat shapes. Larisch's principles of positive and negative space had a great influence on Moser, prompting him to pay particular attention to the disposition of the image upon the sheet. The idea of merging foreground and background especially appealed to him, and he toyed with optical illusions that to some extent anticipate the later work of M. C. Escher (fig. 172). This taste for formal experimentation led Moser to seek more overtly geomet-

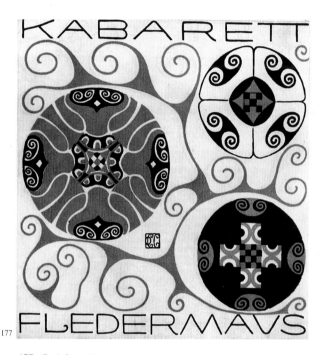

177

177. Carl Otto Czeschka. Program for the Cabaret Fledermaus. 1907. Color lithograph. 9⅝″ × 9¼″. Printed by August Chwala for the Wiener Werkstätte.

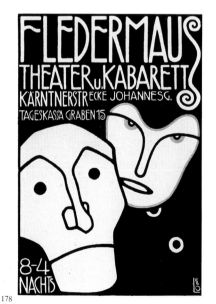

178

179

180

178. Berthold Löffler. Poster designed for the Cabaret Fledermaus. 1907.

179. Carl Otto Czeschka. New Year's greeting. Color lithograph postcard (No. 252). 5½″ × 3½″. Published by the Wiener Werkstätte.

180. Berthold Löffler. Design for a cabaret poster. Ca. 1910. Color lithograph. Published in *Die Fläche*.

ric solutions, and at the height of this phase he interpreted representational forms so exclusively in terms of abstract shape that there is some ambiguity as to which element—the abstract or the representational—is actually dominant (pl. 49). Bold, bright colors, which allude fleetingly if at all to reality, further underscore this abstract treatment. Hoffmann and Moser have been credited with creating two of the first abstract works of art, both done, coincidentally, in conjunction with the 1903 Beethoven exhibition: Moser's was a stained-glass window (fig. 175), Hoffmann's a protocubistic sculptural relief (fig. 174). However bold these formulations may have been for the time, it is misleading to equate them with the abstraction pioneered slightly later by such artists as Picasso or Kandinsky. Hoffmann's and Moser's work was purely ornamental and had none of the moral or expressive fervor of a Kandinsky or a Picasso. That Hoffmann's and Moser's experiments with abstraction led them no further is not surprising, for their work was inherently limited by its decorative purpose. However, the impact of this nascent abstraction on Klimt's development was profound: his almost subjectless landscapes, in which all content is subordinated to the abstract requirements of the picture plane, anticipate the work of the color field painters of the 1960s while at the same time retaining a feeling of mood and place.

The final aspect of Wiener Werkstätte graphic design that related significantly to the fine arts was the decorative/Expressionist phase. Hoffmann believed that "it is the painters who first tread new paths,"[5] and indeed some if not all of the credit for the Wiener Werkstätte's development of a more decorative approach must be given to Klimt. Not only Klimt's much-discussed "gold" paintings, but virtually all of his figural work from the first decade of the century relies on an uneasy combination of ornamental encrustation and three-dimensional realism (pl. 47). This duality has been related by at least one observer to Hoffmann's contrapuntal juxtaposition of flat planes and decorative motifs.[6] A somewhat more trivial adaptation of a Klimtian device may be seen in Wimmer's "Stoclet dress," which actually incorporates the frieze's swirling motif in its embroidery (fig. 176). The new ornamentalism was first brought directly into the Wiener Werkstätte by two artists who joined up around the same time: Carl Otto Czeschka (figs. 177 and 179) and Berthold Löffler (figs. 178 and 180). Czeschka, who headed a master class in painting at the Kunstgewerbeschule and was a former classmate of Moser's, became associated with the Wiener Werkstätte in 1905. Löffler, though essentially a graphic artist, was Michael Powolny's partner at the Wiener Keramik, whose products were distributed by the Werkstätte starting around 1907. Löffler and Czeschka each possessed in equal parts a strong graphic sense and a flair for the decorative—a double interest in playful filigree and in the expressive refinement of flat form. Perhaps most important in the wake of the Werkstätte's purist phase, they both reintroduced the human figure as a representational and aesthetic vehicle in its own right—something that was to be of crucial importance to the emerging Expressionist generation.

Like Art Nouveau/Symbolism and purism/Abstraction, ornamentalism/Expressionism was an influence that worked in two directions. Expressionism proper grew out of the decorative changes in the Werkstätte's graphic style and subsequently returned to haunt the formal schemes of the decadent period. The heightened angularity, as well as the self-conscious naïveté and primitivism of later Werkstätte items, derive from trends that had their start in the early Expressionist years. The rediscovery of folk art—of any expressive forms, including those of children, that were unhampered by the restrictions of formal academic training—was an important component of the modernist move-

181

182

183

181. Rudolf Kalvach. Humorous greeting. Color lithograph postcard (No. 49). 5½″ × 3½″. Published by the Wiener Werkstätte.

182. Ludwig Heinrich Jungnickel. *Parrot Couple*. Color lithograph postcard (No. 376). 5½″ × 3½″. Published by the Wiener Werkstätte.

183. Hans Kalmsteiner. *Puppet Show*. Color lithograph broadsheet (Bilderbogen) (No. 20). 11″ × 7¼″. Published by the Wiener Werkstätte.

ment then developing throughout Europe. In Austria this notion was made all the more relevant by the activities of the pioneering children's art teacher Franz Cizek, who in 1906 began operating an experimental class at the Kunstgewerbeschule. The work of Cizek's child-artists was first exhibited in 1905 at the Österreichisches Museum für Kunst und Industrie, and then at the 1908 Kunstschau. This work was in many ways more competent, and certainly more genuine, than that of the adult artists who would, after the war, try to imitate it.[7]

The various forces of Expressionism first began to coalesce around 1907, a year that proved particularly important for Wiener Werkstätte graphic design. It was in 1907 that the Werkstätte first commenced its postcard series[8] (which would run to approximately a thousand designs published over a period of about seven years) and produced its series of pictorial broadsheets, or *Bilderbogen*. It was also in 1907 that the opening of the Cabaret Fledermaus generated a slew of ancillary graphic arts products. Possibly the postcards and *Bilderbogen* showed the new direction so quickly because, from the start, they were viewed as an appropriate outlet for younger, less experienced artists. Kunstgewerbeschule students were encouraged to create postcard designs, which were relatively inexpensive to produce and required no specialized technical knowledge, and it has been suggested that the *Bilderbogen* originated as a classroom exercise.[9] As the postcard series became established, it was put to a number of practical uses, such as pictorial views of towns or fashion plates (pls. 31 and 32). However, the quality that most distinguishes the designs is a childlike primitivism. Dancing elephants, elves on rats, flying over a cowering cat (fig. 181), animals in costume (fig. 182)—such are the fancies that occupied these artists. Each of the *Bilderbogen* comprised a sequence of vignettes, some of which were also published individually as postcards, that told comic-strip-like tales in a broad, farcical style (fig. 183). The artists used bright, jarring colors and exaggerated, mimelike gestures to strengthen the narrative impact of their little stories. A similar concern with bold forms and simplified expression can be observed in two masklike posters that Löffler designed for the Cabaret Fledermaus (fig. 178) and *Die Fläche* (fig. 180). From here to the forms, colors and gestures of Expressionism was but a short step.

THE FINE ARTS

It may at first glance seem improbable that a style such as Expressionism should emerge from *fin-de-siècle* Austrian design. After all, Expressionism was a fine-art movement, and the Wiener Werkstätte, with its various offshoots, was not. Nor was Austria a nation that had a particularly strong painterly tradition, especially when one considers that Makart's historicism was not a precedent likely to inspire much enthusiasm in the young. The whole ethos of the Wiener Werkstätte was communal; Expressionism was highly individualistic. The Wiener Werkstätte, always interested in decor, was now embarking on its decorative phase; Expressionism was stripped down, bare. So great are the differences between Expressionism and the Werkstätte style that imme-

diately preceded it, it is often assumed that the former was a deliberate rejection of the latter. However, such a statement is at best an oversimplification, for Austria's two leading Expressionists, Oskar Kokoschka and Egon Schiele, both had deep roots in the *fin-de-siècle* tradition.

The only painter who did, systematically and thoroughly, reject the tradition of Klimt and the Wiener Werkstätte was Richard Gerstl, and it may well be that this was due, at least in part, to the same pathological alienation that caused him to take his own life at the age of twenty-five in 1908.[10] Gerstl was perennially at odds with his environment. He broke with his teacher, Heinrich Lefler (the brother-in-law of Josef Urban, who would go on to found the New York branch of the Wiener Werkstätte), because he disapproved of Lefler's participation in the 1908 *Festzug*. He never exhibited, it is said, because he refused to share the Miethke gallery with Gustav Klimt, whom even Kokoschka, at that time, respected. Gerstl had few friends, and no mentors among painters; working alone, he developed a highly idiosyncratic variant of pointillism, in which each dot assumed an expressive, rather than a formalistic significance (fig. 184). In the course of time, the dots turned into sweeping brushstrokes, and the representational subject matter dissolved in a frenzy of emotion-laden paint. Gerstl's late paintings, which are not

184

184. Richard Gerstl. *Self-Portrait with Blue-Green Background*. Ca. 1907. Oil on cardboard. 39¾" × 28⅛".

185. Berthold Löffler. *Madonna*.
1912. Oil on canvas. Signed and
dated, lower right. 41½″ × 37¾″.

186. Berthold Löffler. *Eros*.
Oil on canvas. Signed, lower
right. 32½″ × 30¼″.

unlike those of the Abstract Expressionists, were among the most advanced work being done anywhere in Europe at the time, but as the artist died virtually unknown, they had little immediate influence.

That Gerstl should have developed a strongly Expressionistic style as early as 1905 suggests that the tendency was already very much "in the air."[11] The work of Vincent van Gogh fell under the broad rubric of the 1903 Impressionism exhibition, and was shown again at Miethke in 1906; Edvard Munch's paintings could be seen at the Secession in 1904. Another formative influence was the personal symbolism of the Swiss painter Ferdinand Hodler, long a favorite of the Viennese avant-garde and of particular interest to Moser. However, the various exhibitions of foreign art that the Secession, and later Miethke, mounted may be likened to blood transfusions: they had a revivifying effect, but they were not sustained. With the exodus of the *Klimtgruppe* in 1905, the progressive exhibition program of the Secession all but ceased, and a private gallery such as Miethke could not be expected to mount international cultural exchanges on an institutional scale. By the time Kokoschka and Schiele reached university age, Vienna was slowly sinking back into the cultural isolation from which it had so recently and fitfully begun to emerge.

The indigenous painterly tradition that greeted the youthful Kokoschka and Schiele was not particularly enticing. At the Academy of Fine Arts, historicism still reigned; at the Kunstgewerbeschule, painters created works that were merely fleshed-out versions of the same motifs that appeared on posters and pottery (fig. 186). A dreamy post-Symbolist aestheticism (fig. 185), a predilection for flowers and ornaments—these were the qualities that characterized the paintings of such artists as Löffler. Klimt alone had been successful

in bridging the gulf between historicism and the new decorative trend. The strength and philosophical profundity of his pictorial conceptions are such that even the Stoclet frieze transcends its artsy-craftsy method of execution (pls. 2 and 3, fig. 58). When lesser artists attempted such feats, the result was just the opposite: contact with the applied arts pulled down ostensibly lofty statements to the level of kitsch. Although Moser was one of the more interesting Secessionist painters, he stumbled when confronted with a more demanding commission: the altarpiece (fig. 187) for Otto Wagner's Steinhof church (figs. 26 and 42). Everything went well with Moser's designs for the church's stained-glass windows (fig. 188), but the methods that were appropriate for such essentially decorative panels would not do for an altarpiece. Heinrich Swoboda, who served as spokesman for the church, explained its position as follows: "A window remains, in a manner of speaking, a functional entity, even if it is decorated with figures of saints....But the requirements of an altarpiece, especially this altarpiece, are something else again. An altarpiece is, first and foremost, in content and purpose, simultaneously an aid to and an object of religious worship."[12] Finally, the church rejected Moser's designs, saying, among other things, "These are no angels, but kiss-throwing young girls."[13] Unlike Klimt's university paintings, which had offended by their complexity, Moser's altarpiece offended by its banality.

Lacking strong role models (other than Klimt) among painters, Viennese artists emerging in the first decade of the century were naturally pulled into the orbit of the Wiener Werkstätte. Not only did this group constitute the avant-garde of the day, but it also monopolized a fairly elaborate superstructure linking the studio with the outside world. The Werkstätte circle had established a network that reached out

187

188

187. Koloman Moser. Study for the high altar of the Steinhof church. 1905–06. Tempera.

188. Koloman Moser. *Saint Theresa.* 1905–06. Stained-glass window designed for the Steinhof church, Vienna.

to students at a very early age (practically in infancy, if one counts Cizek's classes), and then guided them throughout their professional careers by organizing exhibitions and coordinating commissions. As long as there was a cadre of wealthy collectors and patrons to fund the enterprise, the superstructure would flourish, and it was a rare artist who, like Gerstl, had enough independent financial support to turn his back on the whole thing.[14] The Wiener Werkstätte was, both stylistically and economically, the cradle in which young artists were nurtured.

It is thus not surprising that the Expressionist explosion came, when it came, from within the ranks of the Wiener Werkstätte's educational arm, the Kunstgewerbeschule. Oskar Kokoschka, then aged eighteen, entered the Kunstgewerbeschule in the autumn of 1904. As prescribed by the curriculum, his first two years were spent in the General Division studying such things as elementary drawing, figure drawing, typography (with Larisch), anatomical drawing, style, and art history.[15] He also took a special preliminary course for teachers-in-training, for it was his original intention to become not an artist, but an art instructor. However, upon completing his term in the General Division, he elected (apparently against his father's wishes) to transfer to Czeschka's master classes in painting. Kokoschka's own descriptions of his Kunstgewerbeschule years, related some forty-five years after the fact, tend to exaggerate the uniqueness of his contributions, when in fact his work was not, initially, all that different from what his classmates were doing. "The entire

Vienna Kunstgewerbeschule," he declared, "was oriented towards ornamentation. Nothing but weeds and flowers and tendrils writhing about like worms. To draw the human figure was taboo. Of course I rebelled against that."[16] It is not clear exactly what Kokoschka meant by "weeds and flowers and tendrils"—certainly not the Art Nouveau style, which was already passé and had never, in any case, had a firm foothold at the Kunstgewerbeschule. While both Czeschka and Löffler (who took over Czeschka's class in 1907, when he went to teach in Hamburg) favored a decorative, flowery style, their work also placed a definite emphasis on the human figure. Kokoschka himself had already been exposed to courses in figure drawing and anatomy. Though he claimed to have introduced the practice of live-action drawing when he was hired as a part-time teaching assistant in 1906, it was

189

189. Rudolf Kalvach. *Abundance*. Color lithograph postcard (No. 106). 5½" × 3½". Published by the Wiener Werkstätte.

190. Oskar Kokoschka. *The Girl Li and I*. Ca. 1906–08. Color lithograph. 9½" × 11⅜". Illustration for *Die träumenden Knaben* (The Dreaming Boys), published by the Wiener Werkstätte.

190

actually Roller who, in 1901, had first devised this method "to transform motion by capturing the moving model with rhythmic strokes—to create an impression with simple means, not tiresome rendering of details, but the essentials of appearance."[17]

A figural revival was already well under way at the Kunstgewerbeschule, and the work of Kokoschka's fellow classmates, reproduced on the postcards and *Bilderbogen* of 1907, evidences concerns very similar to those of Kokoschka's landmark fairy tale, *Die träumenden Knaben*, apparently created the same year.[18] The close relationship between this book and the sentiments already prevalent at the Kunstgewerbeschule is attested to by the fact that one of Kokoschka's classmates actually accused him of plagiarizing the idea.[19] That Kokoschka had, during his student years, a strongly imitative bent is further confirmed by Czeschka's description of him: "I assigned Kokoschka to a big table, by the window. His neighbor was [Rudolf] Kalvach—a strong artistic personality, firmly established, but inferior. Soon Kokoschka was doing the same things as Kalvach! God! I had to gradually convince Kokoschka that such imitation was leading him in a completely false direction—that one must not do that, but find one's own inner path."[20] Kalvach had a child's sense of humor, embarrassingly obvious and a little grotesque. Certain aspects of his style—the use of jarring, posterlike colors and the element of exaggeration (fig. 189)—surface in Kokoschka's early work, tempered by a more typically Viennese elegance.

That Kokoschka did, by and by, find his "own inner path" is amply demonstrated by *Die träumenden Knaben*, even if the book was not as wholly original as has sometimes been suggested (fig. 190). *Die träumenden Knaben* was published by the Wiener Werkstätte in 1908, to coincide with the first Kunstschau. The book was not successful—something the Werkstätte had already anticipated when it failed to get financial support for the project. But, as Wärndorfer explained in a letter to Czeschka, "The Kokoschka thing is so interesting that we will certainly print it, although God knows we have no money."[21] *Die träumenden Knaben* proved to be a *Gesamtkunstwerk* in a vein not previously mined by the Wiener Werkstätte: unified not just in style, but in content. The text, written by Kokoschka himself (an obscure fantasy verging on nightmare), vied for dominance with the colorful but subliminally disturbing imagery, which could hardly be called conventional illustration. This was the new *Gesamtkunstwerk*, in which the elements, rather than being subordinated one to the other, each adhered, independently and equally, to a larger overriding theme. Arnold Schoenberg followed the same general principle in setting poetry to music and in composing his two musical dramas, *Erwartung* (Expectation) and *Die Glückliche Hand* (The Lucky Hand).[22] It is in fact quite possible that the idea for Schoenberg's two stage pieces could have come directly from Kokoschka, whose *Mörder, Hoffnung der Frauen* (Murderer, Hope of Women), performed at the 1909 Kunstschau, is frequently cited as the first Expressionist drama. The new incarnation of the *Gesamt-*

191

191. Oskar Kokoschka.
Dents du Midi. 1909. Oil on
canvas. Initialed, lower right.
29⅞″ × 45⅝″.

192. Egon Schiele. *Portrait of
Poldi Lodzinsky.* 1908. Oil on
canvas. Signed and dated,
lower left. 42⅞″ × 14⅛″.

192

kunstwerk in an artistic rather than a merely decorative guise was symptomatic of the breaking down of the old order and the coming of the new.

The 1908 Kunstschau may, in retrospect, be viewed as a watershed in the history of early-twentieth-century Austrian art. Here all the fashions and forces in the making met, in some cases for the first and only time, thereafter to go their separate ways. This, and the 1909 Kunstschau, constituted the last hurrah of the *Klimtgruppe.* There would be no more grand exhibitions of avant-garde art, foreign or domestic, until after the war. The 1908 Kunstschau was a survey of the state of the arts in Austria. Works in all media, and by artists of all ages (including Kunstgewerbeschule students and even Cizek's children), were shown. The tolerance and outright support that the older generation gave to the new was highly unusual and may in part be explained by the close ties that many of the established artists had with the Kunstgewerbe-schule. Not only did the Wiener Werkstätte court economic disaster by publishing Kokoschka's work,[23] but Klimt actually risked jeopardizing the entire Kunstschau to exhibit it. Kokoschka's contributions, controversial though they were at the time, remain difficult to document, for little other than *Die träumenden Knaben* has survived. Apparently the creation that caused his corner to be dubbed a "Chamber of Horrors" by the ever-eloquent Viennese press was a garishly painted portrait sculpture. Adolf Loos, whose dismay at the new decorative turn taken by the Wiener Werkstätte would prompt him to write his seminal essay, "Ornament and Crime," saw a glimmer of hope in Kokoschka's sculpted head and acquired it for his own collection.

The details of Loos's early relationship with Kokoschka, in particular its exact timing, remain vague, but both men agreed on one thing: it was Loos who caused Kokoschka to break, once and for all, with the Wiener Werkstätte, and who turned him into a painter. As Loos recalled:

> I was told that he was an employee of the Wiener Werkstätte and was busying himself painting fans, designing postcards and such things in the German [i.e. *Jugendstil*] manner—art in the service of commerce. It was immediately clear to me that a great crime against the Holy Ghost was being perpetrated here. So I summoned him. He came.... I promised him the same income if he would leave the Wiener Werkstätte, and I sought commissions for him.[24]

Loos made good on his promise, and between 1909 and 1914, Kokoschka painted almost all the architect's closest friends. Loos also brought him to Switzerland, and here Kokoschka not only painted a number of portraits, but also his first landscape (fig. 191).

Although Kokoschka's claim that painting was not taught at the Kunstgewerbeschule[25] is not borne out by the facts, it is evident that neither Czeschka nor Moser broached the subject in a conventional manner. Certainly Kokoschka's experiences with tempera and poster paint did not prepare him to handle oils, nor was his new assignment, portraiture, anything he had encountered in the classroom. Rather than being a handicap, however, Kokoschka's lack of training as a painter proved an asset. He used oil paint in a way that no academically educated artist would have, and he interpreted his subjects in an entirely personal and unique manner (pl. 55). Instead of systematically building his forms, he applied the paint and then scraped away at it, allowing the texture of raw canvas to rise through to the surface. Instead of flattering

193

193. Egon Schiele. *Portrait of
the Painter Anton Peschka.*
1909. Oil on canvas. Signed
and dated, lower left.
43¼″ × 39¼″.

the personalities of his sitters, he exposed them; instead of decorating, he revealed. Comparison of Kokoschka's poster for the 1909 Kunstschau (pl. 52) with that done the previous year (fig. 4) shows just how far he had traveled in this short time.

·At the 1909 Kunstschau, Kokoschka encountered, not at all happily, a challenger to the title of "*Oberwildling*" (Super Fauve), which he himself had so recently claimed as his own. The challenger, Egon Schiele, was still a student at the Academy, and in keeping with this more painterly background, where Kokoschka's dominant influence had been the Wiener Werkstätte, his was Klimt. In fact, after his Kunstschau debut, he was known briefly as the "Silver Klimt." As is suggested by this epithet, Schiele's early work (fig. 193), though not entirely conventional, was not nearly as radical as Kokoschka's. However, in part under the influence of Kokoschka and of the foreign art that was included in the 1909 exhibition, he soon departed decisively from the Klimtian tradition.

Schiele's breakthrough to an Expressionist idiom, which came in 1910, at first glance resembles a plunge into the void after a surfeit of decoration. Upon further reflection it becomes evident that this void was always implicit in the *horror vacui* not just of Klimt's paintings, but also of much Wiener Werkstätte graphic design. It is, after all, this void that is being filled; what Schiele did was merely to remove the fill, thereby exposing his subject (pl. 54). In his careful disposition of negative space, and in his acute awareness of the edges of the picture plane, he retained the graphic tension that had informed the work of his predecessors. Like Kokoschka, Schiele was not a painter in the conventional

sense, and though both men executed phenomenal paintings, Schiele's method remained essentially graphic; oil is often handled more like watercolor and is subordinated to a strong underlying drawing. Schiele's debt to the Wiener Werkstätte made itself felt not only in his art, but also in little details such as his stylized signature, his preference for Hoffmann frames, and in the massive black rectilinear furniture that he designed for his studio.

After Schiele, bolstered by his debut at the 1909 Kunstschau, decided to drop out of the Academy, he naturally turned to the Wiener Werkstätte, which seemed to consider one of its duties to provide employment for needy artists. Just as the Werkstätte had helped Kokoschka by buying his work, publishing his book and postcard designs, and giving him little commissions, they were perfectly ready to count Schiele in on their various projects. The postcards that Schiele created specifically for the Werkstätte were never printed, though some years later a series reproducing three of his watercolors was released. Another unsuccessful assignment involved a stained-glass window for the Palais Stoclet. Schiele's contribution—supposedly the ungainly *Portrait of Poldi Lodzinsky* (fig. 192)—was rejected for obvious reasons. There was no place for the jarring sentiments of Expressionism in Josef Hoffmann's fantasy palace. However, in Hoffmann's heart, and in the heart of his partner Moser, there seemed infinite room for all young artists. Moser beseeched Klimt to find some way to help Schiele and his contemporaries: "They are all quite excellent youths, full of enthusiasm and with empty pockets; people of whom Austria could one day be proud, but who meanwhile are only abused and mocked."[26] Klimt was, in fact, extremely kind to Schiele, supplying him not only with advice, but also with models and even patrons.[27] Hoffmann, too, found Schiele a steady patron: Heinrich Böhler (cousin of the artist Hans Böhler) hired Schiele as a painting teacher and then paid him a monthly allowance throughout the war years. Many was the time that Schiele, perennially short of cash, stopped by the Wiener Werkstätte's shop on the Graben looking for a handout. Whether the Werkstätte ever sold the watercolors and drawings that they acquired in exchange for their largesse is debatable. When one considers that Schiele's work at this time was grounds for arrest in a provincial Austrian town, the assistance of the Wiener Werkstätte seems not only exceptional but pivotal. It is impossible to imagine Schiele or Kokoschka receiving any sort of public encouragement ten years earlier, before the support structure of the Secession and Werkstätte had been established.

In a certain sense the Wiener Werkstätte's purist phase, waning at the time of the Kunstschau, lived on or was reborn in the graphic power and calligraphic gestures, the expressive essences, of Oskar Kokoschka and Egon Schiele. Similarly, both artists continued the tradition of Klimtian symbolism. Whereas Klimt had stripped allegory of its historicist context and in the process had given it a contemporary meaning, Kokoschka and Schiele transformed their own lives into allegories, and in so doing made the personal universal. The sensuality that in Klimt's paintings was cloaked (but by no means concealed), was openly explored by the younger artists: by Kokoschka in semiautobiographical vignettes that related the intricacies of male-female relationships (fig. 195), and by Schiele in depictions of figures who, even when coupling, endure the agonies of their sexuality in solitude (fig. 194). Thus both Kokoschka and Schiele picked up on elements that were always latent in the *fin-de-siècle* aesthetic but that had become increasingly alienated from the later, decorative approach. They brought the artistic back into the realm of art and left the Wiener Werkstätte to its destiny of decadence and decline. As the emphasis of the Werkstätte shifted decisively from functionalism to ornamentalism, from art to the artsy-craftsy, the moral and spiritual force that it abandoned surfaced in the work of the younger generation. These, suddenly, were painters who really painted, instead of designing dish towels or bookcases. And as if acknowledging that the communal spirit had failed, art turned inward again, toward the unique soul of the individual artist.

So it was that in ten short years a group of multitalented artists and designers had brought the Austrian nation all the way from Art Nouveau to Expressionism. This decade—between the founding of the Secession in 1898 and the Kunstschau of 1908—was a period in which a unique combination of circumstances served to make Vienna a vessel for artistic ferment on a scale rarely encountered. More than just a question of the right place and the right time, it was a matter of the right circumstances. The Ringstrasse era of economic and physical growth had turned Vienna into a magnet for artistic (and other) talents from all over the empire. A good

portion of the major *fin-de-siècle* artists were not born in Vienna, and of the rest, most were no better than second-generation Viennese. The growth of a newly rich upper middle class, educated during the Ring era and willing to assume, upon maturity, the role of patron as a social mandate, provided the economic base that the Secession and the Wiener Werkstätte required. In the development of an autonomous middle class, as in the development of industry, Austria lagged behind many of her Western European neighbors. Perhaps for this reason, many of the innovations that came to Vienna at the turn of the century arrived a bit later than they had in other countries. Vienna was late in formulating a Secession movement, late in founding an artists' journal and, finally, late in establishing a crafts collective. Because all these wonderful innovations reached Vienna only at the turn of the century, it was possible to apply them to a new and more modern era than had, for example, greeted the original British crafts revival of the nineteenth century. And because these innovations came more or less at the same time, their effects could be applied cumulatively. Had the Austro-Hungarian empire not been destroyed by World War I, the Wiener Werkstätte might yet have fulfilled its early promise, and the emergent talents of the prewar period might have lived on to blossom forth and bear fruit. As it is, we are left with a truncated nation, long eclipsed by the dark shadow of Germany, and a magical "golden age" that seems more like a dream than the reality it truly was.

194

195

194. Egon Schiele. *Embracing Couple*. 1914. Black crayon on paper. Signed and dated, lower right. 19½″ × 12⅞″.

195. Oskar Kokoschka. *Nude Couple*. 1914. Lithograph. 9½″ × 6¼″. Illustration for *Allos Makar*.

47. Gustav Klimt. *Judith I.*
1901. Oil on canvas, in a gold
frame designed by the artist or
his brother, Georg. Signed,
lower left. 33⅛″ × 16½″.

48. Koloman Moser. Poster for
Frommes Kalender. 1898.
Color lithograph. 37½″ × 24½″.
Printed by Albert Berger.

49

50

50. Patterns and decorative
motifs. Ca. 1903–04. Color
lithograph. Published in *Die
Fläche*.

49. Koloman Moser. Poster for
the thirteenth Secession exhibition. 1902. Color lithograph.
37⅜″ × 12⅜″. Printed by Albert
Berger.

51

51. Oskar Kokoschka. *The Hunt*. 1907–08. Tempera on paper. 10″ × 8″.

52. Oskar Kokoschka. *Kunstschau 1908*. Color lithograph
poster. 37⅜″ × 25″. Printed by
Albert Berger.

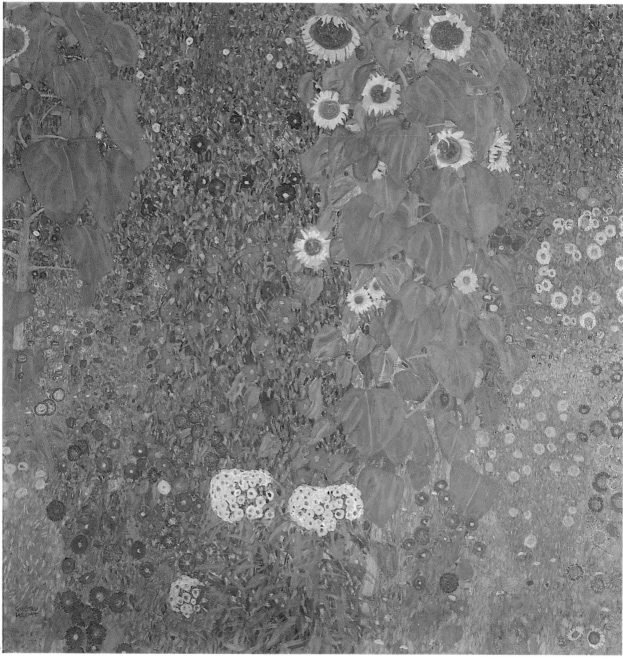

53. Gustav Klimt. *Farm Garden with Sunflowers.* Ca. 1905–
06. Oil on canvas. Signed, lower
left. 43¼" × 43¼".

54

54. Egon Schiele. *Sunflowers*.
1911. Oil on canvas. Signed and
dated, lower left. 35½″ × 31¾″.

55

55. Oskar Kokoschka. *Lotte Franzos*. 1908–09. Oil on canvas. Initialed, lower right. 44⅞″ × 33½″.

CHRONOLOGY

The story of the Wiener Werkstätte, with its complex interweaving of characters and events, cries out for explication by means of a chronology. However, the preparation of such a chronology is hindered by the vagueness that surrounds many of the dates and activities involved. Artists drifted in and out of the Wiener Werkstätte and the Artists' Workshops, and in many cases no documents survive to pinpoint the exact dates or terms of employment even of principal figures. To further complicate matters, existing sources sometimes provide contradictory dates for the same event. In compiling this chronology, an attempt has been made to establish the dates that, based on present research, seem most logical or correct. Further research may prove that one item or another is off by a year or so, but this will not seriously undermine the purpose of the chronology: to provide an overview of the flow of change that constitutes the history of the Wiener Werkstätte.

1897

Klimt and a group of relatively progressive artists secede from the Künstlerhaus, which runs the only Viennese exhibition facility for contemporary art. Later that year the Secession is given a site on which to construct its own building by the City of Vienna. Von Scala is named director of the Österreichisches Museum für Kunst und Industrie, ushering in a more liberal era. In Darmstadt, Koch begins publishing in *Deutsche Kunst und Dekoration*.

1898

The Secession holds its first exhibition in rented quarters and, later that year, inaugurates its new building. It also publishes the first issue of its journal, *Ver Sacrum*. Hoffmann receives a teaching post at the Kunstgewerbeschule, and Klimt receives a commission to paint three allegorical panels for the University of Vienna.

1899

Moser begins teaching at the Kunstgewerbeschule; Olbrich, architect of the Secession building, fails to get a teaching post there and instead leaves Vienna for the artists' colony of Mathildenhöhe, outside Darmstadt.

1900

The Secession mounts a major exhibition of international design, including work by Ashbee, Mackintosh and van de Velde. Moser exhibits his first furniture, and Hoffmann begins work on the Hohe Warte villa colony on the outskirts of Vienna. Klimt's first university painting creates a scandal in Vienna but is awarded a prize at the Paris World's Fair, where the exhibitions of Austrian applied arts (installed by Hoffmann) also win special praise.

1901

Members of Hoffmann's and Moser's first class of Kunstgewerbeschule graduates exhibit with the Wiener Kunstgewerbeverein under the name *Wiener Kunst im Hause*.

1902

The Austrian Ministry of Education sends Myrbach and Hoffmann to study schools in England. Czeschka begins teaching at the Kunstgewerbeschule. The Beethoven exhibition at the Secession combines sculpture, painting, architecture and music in a total environment.

1903

The Wiener Werkstätte is founded by Hoffmann and Moser with financial backing from Wärndorfer. At first it occupies a small apartment on the Heumühlgasse, but then it moves to permanent quarters on the Neustiftgasse, containing workshops for metalwork, leatherwork, bookbinding, and a paint shop. *Ver Sacrum* ceases regular publication. Otto Wagner begins work on the Steinhof church (1903-07).

1904

The Wiener Werkstätte receives, among its early commissions, the assignment to build the Purkersdorf Sanatorium (1904-05), and to prepare a commemorative publication for the hundredth anniversary of the Österreichische Staatsdruckerei. A woodworking shop is added (in operation until ca. 1907/08). The Werkstätte has its first exhibition at the Hohenzollern Kunstgewerbehaus in Berlin, and *Deutsche Kunst und Dekoration* publishes its first article on the Werkstätte. Hoffmann's friend Lux founds the journal *Hohe Warte*. Moser begins work on the stained-glass windows and altarpiece for the Steinhof church. Klimt's friend Bacher buys the Galerie Miethke and Moll takes over as artistic adviser.

1905

The Wiener Werkstätte is included in the itinerary of the *Wiener Kunstwanderungen* (art tours) and publishes a formal work program. It prints its first textiles and has its first Viennese exhibition (consisting of bookbindings) at the Galerie Miethke. Czeschka becomes active in the Werkstätte and designs its first postcard. Work begins on the Palais Stoclet (1905-11). Klimt renounces the university commission; he and his associates secede from the Secession.

1906

A new showroom is added to the Neustiftgasse premises and inaugurated with the exhibition "The Laid Table." Powolny and Löffler found the Wiener Keramik.

1907

The Wiener Werkstätte opens its first showroom in downtown Vienna, on the Graben, and takes over distribution for the Wiener Keramik. It begins publication of its postcard series and also designs the Cabaret Fledermaus. Moser leaves to devote more time to painting. Czeschka accepts a teaching post in Hamburg, and Löffler takes over his class at the Kunstgewerbeschule. The Werkstätte becomes a founding member of the Deutscher Werkbund.

1908

To commemorate the sixtieth anniversary of Emperor Franz Josef's reign, a mammoth *Festzug* (festival parade) and exhibition, the Kunstschau, are arranged. The Wiener Werkstätte publishes a series of commemorative postcards as well as Kokoschka's book *Die träumenden Knaben*; Kokoschka makes his debut at the Kunstschau.

1909

A second Kunstschau includes work by Schiele as well as Kokoschka. Powolny begins teaching at the Kunstgewerbeschule. The Wiener Werkstätte opens a full-fledged textile division.

1910

An experimental fashion division, under Wimmer's direction, is opened at the Werkstätte's Karlsbad branch. Hoffmann and Lobmeyr collaborate on glassware.

1911

International exhibition in Rome. The fashion department receives an official license to operate and opens premises next to the Werkstätte's Graben showroom.

1912

The fashion department scores its first decisive success at the Hohenzollern Kunstgewerbehaus in Berlin. Wimmer begins teaching at the Kunstgewerbeschule.

1913

The Artists' Workshops begin operation on the Döblergasse, in a building built and owned by Wagner. The Wiener Keramik merges with the Gmundner Keramik. The Österreichisches Museum für Kunst und Industrie organizes a wallpaper exhibition. Founding of the Österreichischer Werkbund. With an outstanding debt of 1.5 million kronen, the Werkstätte temporarily halts production.

1914

Archduke Franz Ferdinand is assassinated in Sarajevo and World War I begins. The Wiener Werkstätte is liquidated and reorganized as a privately held corporation (*Gesellschaft mit beschränkter Haftung*); the Primavesis become the largest stockholders. The fashion department is granted "factory" status and moves to enlarged quar-

ters on the Johannesgasse. Deutscher Werkbund exhibition in Cologne. Publication of *Mode Wien 1914/15*.

1915

New main offices are opened on the Tegetthoffstrasse. Primavesi becomes managing director. Peche becomes manager of the Artists' Workshops. The Wiener Werkstätte begins to produce hand-painted glassware. Fashion exhibition at the Österreichisches Museum.

1916

At Peche's request, an ivory workshop is added. The fashion department opens a showroom in the Palais Esterhazy on the Kärntnerstrasse. Emperor Franz Josef dies and is succeeded by his nephew, Karl.

1917

Branches in Marienbad and Zürich (supervised by Peche) and a textile shop on the Kärntnerstrasse near the fashion showroom are opened. The Artists' Workshops begin producing ceramics.

1918

Klimt, Schiele, and Moser die. The war ends, as does the Habsburg monarchy; proclamation of the Austrian Republic.

1919

Peche returns from Zürich and becomes artistic director of the Wiener Werkstätte. Max Schmidt brings out the first Peche wallpaper collection. Equipment for glass cutting and engraving is acquired. The fashion showroom in the Palais Esterhazy is enlarged.

1920

A Kunstschau commemorates the dead; the Wiener Werkstätte is criticized for being out of touch with the times. Häusler attempts to reorganize the Werkstätte along more practical lines. The Zürich branch closes.

1921

A New York branch is opened by the stage designer and architect Urban.

1922

A branch is opened in Velden. Wimmer goes to America, and Snischek and Likarz take over the fashion department.

1923

Peche dies and is succeeded by Zimpel.

BIBLIOGRAPHY

1924

The fashion department is constituted as an independent entity, the Modehaus der Wiener Werkstätte Primavesi & Co. The New York branch folds.

1925

Zimpel dies. Häusler quits. Wimmer returns from America and resumes his post at the Kunstgewerbeschule but not at the Wiener Werkstätte. The Werkstätte is attacked because of its poor showing at the Paris Art Deco exhibition.

1926

Primavesi dies and his bank collapses. The Wiener Werkstätte becomes a publicly held corporation (*Aktiengesellschaft*).

1927

The fashion department is reabsorbed into the company as a whole. Grohmann takes over as manager of the Werkstätte.

1928

The Wiener Werkstätte celebrates its twenty-fifth anniversary.

1929

A Berlin branch opens and is an immediate failure; an attempt to revive the New York branch likewise fails. Salubra brings out the Flögl wallpaper collection.

1930

The silver workshop is closed. Grohmann resigns. Hofmann and Oeri acquire the stock of the Werkstätte.

1931

The fashion department closes its showroom in the Palais Esterhazy and moves in with the textile division. The workshop operation is terminated and liquidation of the inventory begins.

1932

The Wiener Werkstätte's remaining inventory is liquidated in September, and the fashion department's in November.

1939

The name Wiener Werkstätte is removed from the trade registry and its archives donated to the Österreichisches Museum für Kunst und Industrie.

The following books have been used as principal sources and will not be cited unless there is a factual discrepancy or specific passages are quoted:

Baroni, Daniele, and Antonio D'Auria. *Josef Hoffmann und die Wiener Werkstätte*. Stuttgart: Deutsche Verlags-Anstalt, 1984.

Behal, Vera J. *Möbel des Jugendstils*. Munich: Prestel Verlag, 1981.

Fenz, Werner. *Koloman Moser, Graphik, Kunstgewerbe, Malerei*. Salzburg: Residenz Verlag, 1984.

Gebogenes Holz, Konstruktive Entwürfe Wien 1840–1910. Vienna: Julius Hummel and Stefan Asenbaum, 1979.

Koloman Moser, 1868–1918. Vienna: Hochschule für angewandte Kunst, 1979.

Neuwirth, Waltraud. *Josef Hoffmann, Bestecke für die Wiener Werkstätte*. Vienna: Selbstverlag Dr. Waltraud Neuwirth, 1982.

_____. *Die Keramik der Wiener Werkstätte I*. Vienna: Selbstverlag Dr. Waltraud Neuwirth, 1981.

_____. *Österreichische Keramik des Jugendstils*. Munich: Prestel Verlag, 1974.

_____. *Wiener Werkstätte, Avantgarde, Art Déco, Industrial Design*. Vienna: Selbstverlag Dr. Waltraud Neuwirth, 1984.

Schweiger, Werner J. *Wiener Werkstätte, Design in Vienna 1903–1932*. New York: Abbeville Press, 1984.

Sekler, Eduard F. *Josef Hoffmann, The Architectural Work*. Princeton: Princeton University Press, 1985.

Völker, Angela. *Wiener Mode und Modefotografie, Die Modeabteilung der Wiener Werkstätte 1911–1932*. Munich/Paris: Verlag Schneider-Henn, 1984.

FOOTNOTES

INTRODUCTION

1. Waltraud Neuwirth, *Österreichische Keramik des Jugendstils* (Munich: Prestel Verlag, 1974), p. 78.

I. BACKGROUND

1. Koloman Moser, "Vom Schreibtisch und aus dem Atelier: Mein-Werdegang," in *Koloman Moser 1868–1918* (Vienna: Hochschule für angewandte Kunst, 1979), p. 9.
2. Hugo Haberfeld, "The Architectural Revival in Austria," in *The Studio*, 1906, p. (C) ii.
3. Adolf Loos, "Potemkin's Town" (1898), in *Vienna Moderne: 1898–1918* (Houston: Sarah Campbell Blaffer Gallery, 1979), p. 86.
4. Otto Wagner, "Moderne Architektur" (1896), in *Vienna: Turn of the Century Art and Design* (London: Fischer Fine Art, Ltd., 1979), p. 4.
5. Eduard F. Sekler, *Josef Hoffmann: The Architectural Work* (Princeton: Princeton University Press, 1985), p. 13.
6. For a detailed discussion of the events leading up to the founding of the Secession, see James Schedel, *Art and Society: The New Art Movement in Vienna, 1897–1914* (Palo Alto: The Society for the Promotion of Science, 1981).
7. In view of its eventual role and the general stylistic thrust of its membership, the Secession may be considered the avant-garde of its time and place, with the proviso that it was interested far more in a general ideal of creative freedom than in promoting any one style. Its earliest members included Hoffmann, Klimt, Olbrich, Moll, and Moser. Rudolf von Alt, then almost ninety and one of the most esteemed artists of the Biedermeier period, was appointed honorary president; Wagner joined up relatively late, in 1899.
8. Peter Vergo, *Art in Vienna, 1898–1918* (London: Phaidon Press, Ltd., 1975), p. 23.
9. *Ver Sacrum*, Vol. I, No. 1 (January 1898), p. 9.
10. A certain portion of the Secession's proceeds (like the Künstler-haus, it took a 10 percent commission on all sales) was to be used for the acquisition of modern art. Otto Wagner designed a museum to house these works, but it was never built. Instead the collection was eventually given provisional quarters in the Belve-dere Palace, where, with some adjustments and administrative changes, the bulk of it remains to this day.
11. *Ver Sacrum*, Vol. I, No. 1 (January 1898), p. 6.
12. Today the Österreichisches Museum für angewandte Kunst.
13. In 1909 the South Kensington Museum split into the Science Museum and the Victoria and Albert Museum.
14. Today the Hochschule für angewandte Kunst.
15. Scala's initial winter exhibition, in 1897/98, was the first to display "modern" interiors by designers such as Josef Urban and Heinrich Lefler. However, Scala's anglophilia went too far for the Secession-ists' tastes, and when he began to actively encourage native indus-try to copy British models (as was, after all, in keeping with the museum's long-standing policy) he was roundly attacked by the avant-garde.
16. Most of the teachers were employed on a provisional basis before being named professors; Hoffmann's official appointment came in 1899, Moser's in 1900.
17. The influence of the Secession and the Wiener Werkstätte on the Kunstgewerbeschule is so far-reaching that it is difficult to pinpoint an exact termination date. Eduard Josef Wimmer-Wisgrill taught there until 1953, Hilda Jesser until 1967.
18. Alessandra Comini, *Egon Schiele's Portraits* (Berkeley: University of California Press, 1974), p. 19.
19. For a detailed discussion of Mackintosh's influence on Hoffmann, see Sekler, pp. 39-40.
20. Roger Billcliffe, *Mackintosh Furniture* (New York: E. P. Dutton, 1984), p. 69. Billcliffe cites the Westdel house in Glasgow as the first use of the square motif. Interestingly, this project was first published in 1902 in the German journal *Dekorative Kunst*.
21. Billcliffe (p. 69) states that only two pieces by Mackintosh were sold at the Secession exhibition: an armchair, to Moser, and a cabi-net, to Hugo Henneberg (around which Hoffmann would design a room in Henneberg's Hohe Warte villa).
22. Gottfried Semper was probably most instrumental in transmitting the British lesson to the German-speaking world. His essay "Wis-senschaft, Industrie und Kunst," published in 1852 in direct response to the Great Exhibition in London the year before, was one of the earliest attempts to deal with the aesthetic implications of industrialization.
23. Carl E. Schorske, *Fin-de-Siècle Vienna, Politics and Culture* (New York: Alfred A. Knopf, 1980), p. 304.
24. Jane Kallir, *Arnold Schoenberg's Vienna* (New York: Rizzoli International Publications, 1984), p. 73. All of these men felt that the aristocrat's imperative and the artist's imperative were allied.
25. Walter Gropius, "Programme of the Staatliche Bauhaus in Wei-mar" (1919), in *Vienna Moderne*, p. 91.
26. Isabelle Anscombe and Charlotte Gere, *Arts & Crafts in Britain and America* (New York: Rizzoli International Publications, 1978), p. 110.
27. Otto Wagner, Jr., "Josef M. Olbrich, ein Nachruf," in *Deutsche Bauzeitung*, Vol. XLII, August 15, 1908, p. 456.
28. *Die Kunst und die Revolution* (1849), *Das Kunstwerk der Zukunft* (1849), and *Oper und Drama* (1851).
29. Gropius in *Vienna Moderne*, p. 91.
30. For a detailed discussion of the Austrian *Gesamtkunstwerk*, see Werner Hofmann, "Gesamtkunstwerk Wien," in *Der Hang zum Gesamtkunstwerk* (Zürich: Kunsthaus Zürich, 1983), pp. 84-92.
31. Sekler, p. 33.
32. Vergo, p. 164.
33. This story has long been part of the Wiener Werkstätte legend, though its accuracy has recently been challenged by Werner Sch-weiger (*Wiener Werkstätte, Design in Vienna 1903–1932* [New York: Abbeville Press, 1984], p. 91), who contends that Wimmer made his first visit to the Stoclets only in 1912, a year after the fashion department formally opened. In any case, the spirit of the anecdote remains accurate enough.

II. HISTORY

1. In 1892 the Munich Secession was founded, and within the next three years similar splits had divided the artistic populations of Düsseldorf, Weimar, Dresden and Karlsruhe. Vienna, in 1897, and Berlin, in 1898, were the two last major cities to form Secession movements. Berlin, however, differed from Vienna in that it had a well-developed network of commercial galleries, and almost from the start its Secession established close ties with these dealers.

2. Prior to 1904 the Galerie Miethke (founded in 1861 by Hugo Othmar Miethke) represented conservative nineteenth-century art in the Ringstrasse mode. After Klimt's friend Paul Bacher bought the gallery in 1904, Moll took over as artistic director and the exhibition program became far more progressive.

3. The money to reclaim Klimt's university paintings was provided by the wealthy industrialist August Lederer and by Kolomon Moser, who divided the works between them.

4. According to Nora Wärndorfer Hodges (the daughter of August Wärndorfer; interview, January 23, 1986), the family name was spelled with an umlaut over the *a*. However, upon joining the Wiener Werkstätte, Fritz Wärndorfer adopted the alternative spelling "Waerndorfer." This spelling was consistent with the style popular with many Werkstätte artists (the word Werkstätte was, in fact, spelled with an *ae* in the organization's original logo). This preference may have a typographical explanation, in that the umlaut, rising above the other letters, disrupts the unity of a line of type. For the sake of consistency, the umlauted *a* is used throughout this book.

5. Both Leopold Wolfgang Rochowanski (*Josef Hoffmann, Eine Studie geschrieben zu seinem 80. Geburtstag*, [Vienna: Verlag der Österreichischen Staatsdruckerei, 1950]) and Hoffmann himself ("Selbstbiographie" in *Ver Sacrum—Neue Folge 4* [Vienna/Munich: Verlag für Jugend und Volk, 1972]) contend that the idea of the Wiener Werkstätte was first mooted at the Café Heinrichshof in late 1902 or early 1903. Moser and Hoffmann were sitting with Wagner, Wärndorfer and some friends griping about the artistic situation in Vienna, when Wärndorfer asked what it would cost to finance such a venture. Moser and Hoffmann took him up on his offer, and so, supposedly, the Wiener Werkstätte was born.

6. Werner J. Schweiger, *Wiener Werkstätte, Design in Vienna 1903-1932* (New York: Abbeville Press, 1984), p. 16.

7. The original members of *Wiener Kunst im Hause*—Gisela von Falke, Emil Holzinger, Franz Messner, Marietta Peyfuss, William Schmidt, Jutta Sika, Karl Sumetsberger, Therese Trethan, Else Unger and Hans Vollmer—were later joined by Yvonne Brick, Agnes Hossner and Alexandra von Sauer-Csaky.

8. According to Nora Hodges (interview, January 3, 1986), Fritz Wärndorfer's father had been a cofounder of the firm of Wärndorfer, Benedict, Mautner, which had several factories in Bohemia and one in Lower Austria. The second generation consisted of two Wärndorfer sons, Fritz and August, and two Mautner sons, Stefan and Konrad, who collectively bought out the Benedict family's interest and changed the company's name to Österreichisches Textilwerk. The oft-repeated assertion that Wärndorfer was involved in banking is incorrect.

9. According to Nora Hodges (see above), both Fritz and August Wärndorfer were sent to England to study the British textile industry before entering the family business; the family also had British relatives.

10. It is Nora Hodges's contention that almost none of the second-generation proprietors of the family firm was particularly interested in it, and that Fritz Wärndorfer was able to devote almost all his time to the Wiener Werkstätte.

11. Schweiger, pp. 42-43.

12. Many sources imply that the cabinetry shop was part of the Wiener Werkstätte from the beginning, but in fact it was only officially authorized in 1904. Woodworking, with its noise and machinery, was somewhat different in scale from the other crafts workshops; the neighbors complained, and the cabinetry shop was forced to suspend operations in 1907 or 1908.

13. Other than a cabinet in the entry hall and some metal desk accessories, no contributions by Moser to the Palais Stoclet have thus far been documented.

14. Josef Hoffmann, "Unser Weg zum Menschentum, 25 Jahre Wiener Werkstätte," in *Deutsche Kunst und Dekoration*, Vol. LXII, August 1928. According to this statement, woven and printed fabrics, carpets and wallpaper were produced by outside licensees; all other items were manufactured on the premises of the Wiener Werkstätte.

15. Robert Cole, one of the biographers of Josef Urban, has so far been unable to confirm the date when Urban opened the Wiener Werkstätte's New York branch. The first articles on the branch, published in *The New York Times* in June 1922, suggest that the shop was opened only that year. The 1921 date derives from an article on Urban published in *Architecture Magazine* in May 1934.

16. The Österreichischer Werkbund, which held its first official meeting in the spring of 1913, from the start placed far less emphasis on industrial production than did its German counterpart. After the war, Hoffmann criticized the Österreichischer Werkbund for promoting sloppy workmanship and was consequently attacked for conflict of interest. As a result, the Werkbund split in 1920, and Hoffmann founded his own "Werkbund Wien." Sporadic attempts to reconcile the two groups were made throughout the 1920s.

17. Waltraud Neuwirth (*Österreichische Keramik des Jugendstils* [Munich: Prestel Verlag, 1974], p. 209) gives 1905 as the date of the founding of the Wiener Keramik; Schweiger (p. 263) gives the date as 1906.

18. Otto Wagner constructed the building on the Döblergasse in 1912 and leased a portion of it to the Artists' Workshops that year; the workshops probably began to operate in 1913.

19. Schweiger, pp. 42-43.

20. Peter Vergo, *Art in Vienna, 1898-1918* (London: Phaidon Press, Ltd., 1975), p. 132.

21. J. A. Lux, "Wiener Werkstätte, Josef Hoffmann, Koloman Moser," in *Deutsche Kunst und Dekoration*, Vol. XV, 1904/05, p. 7.

22. Schweiger, p. 113.

23. Ibid., p. 42.

24. Ibid., p. 43.

25. Hermann Bahr, "Contrefaçon, Epilog zur Winterausstellung des Österreichischen Museums," in *Sezession*, 1900, p. 188. In his essay, Bahr also wondered "out loud" whether such copying was actually permissible: "Is that allowed? Is there no legal protection against it?" In fact an attempt was made subsequently to apply some sort of legal constraints to the copying then rampant in the Viennese furniture industry, but such practices were so widespread, and had for so long been condoned by the museum itself, that it was very difficult to know where to draw the line.

26. Interview with Mäda Primavesi, December 30, 1985.

27. James Shedel, *Art and Society: The New Art Movement in Vienna, 1897-1914* (Palo Alto: The Society for the Promotion of Science, 1981), p. 56. Shedel seems to have established that Wittgenstein's grant came to 60,000 gulden, which according to Shedel's table of values (p. 209) would equal 120,000 kronen or roughly $25,200.

28. The portrait of Magda Mautner-Markhof was never actually executed.

29. Alessandra Comini, *Egon Schiele's Portraits* (Berkeley: University of California Press, 1974), page 127.

30. Ibid., pp. 127-131. Comini gives the cost of the Klimt portrait as "the equivalent of $7,000" (page 234, note 52), which would have then been 33,600 kronen.

31. Peter Vergo, "Dream and Reality: The Wiener Werkstätte 1903-1913," in *Vienna 1900* (Paris: Centres Georges Pompidou, 1986). Vergo notes that artists were allowed to buy many products at close to cost, further reducing the Werkstätte's income. Hereafter cited as Vergo II.

32. Eduard F. Sekler, *Josef Hoffmann, The Architectural Work* (Princeton: Princeton University Press, 1985), p. 63.

33. Schweiger, p. 42.

34. Like many aspects of the Werkstätte's program, the Artists' Workshops were in reality less than ideal. The royalty setup meant that artists might receive little or no compensation if their work failed to sell, something that became a sore point during the economic distress of the 1920s.

35. Interview with Mäda Primavesi, December 12, 1985.

36. Vergo II.

37. Ludwig Goldscheider, *Kokoschka* (London: Phaidon Press, Ltd., 1963), p. 13.

38. Sekler, p. 76.

39. Koloman Moser, letter to Josef Hoffmann, February 20, 1907, in Werner Fenz, *Koloman Moser* (Salzburg: Residenz Verlag, 1984), p. 249, note 109.

40. Interview with Nora Wärndorfer Hodges, December 20, 1985.

41. Vergo II.

42. Ibid. Vergo also states that "at one point Wärndorfer suddenly, and inexplicably, turns up in London, trying to float the WW as a going concern on the London stock market, but to no avail." Schweiger (p. 96) contends that the Wiener Werkstätte was in fact registered as "Vienna Works Ltd." in England in 1912. As Schweiger notes, it remains to be determined whether this was purely a legal formality or had any larger significance for the parent company in Austria.

43. Schweiger, p. 96. Nora Hodges (interview, January 3, 1986) recalls that the amount was 1,250,000 kronen.

44. Interview with Nora Hodges, December 20, 1985. The family of Fritz Wärndorfer's wife (who remained behind in Austria with the children) also put up some of the money to pay off the Wiener Werkstätte debt. At around this time, and possibly also in connection with the Werkstätte fiasco, the Wärndorfer family sold out the balance of its interest in the Österreichisches Textilwerk.

45. Interview with Mäda Primavesi, December 30, 1985.

46. Josef Urban also organized an American "Artists' Fund" that sent money to needy Austrian artists.

47. Interview with Gretl Urban (Josef Urban's daughter), January 3, 1986. Urban, it is interesting to note, had many extremely wealthy society clients, such as William Randolph Hearst and Marjorie Post, but they did not buy in sufficient quantity to keep the enterprise alive. The kind of comprehensive patronage that was so common in Austria simply did not exist in the vast, democratic United States.

48. Angela Völker (*Wiener Mode und Modefotografie* [Munich/Paris: Verlag Schneider-Henn, 1984], p. 252) states that the Zürich branch closed in 1920, while Schweiger (p. 121) notes that the Wiener Werkstätte A.G. remained in the business registry in Zürich until February 1926.

49. Interview with Mäda Primavesi, December 20, 1985.

50. Interview with Mäda Primavesi, December 30, 1985. Further difficulties were created by the extreme complexity both of Primavesi's other business interests and of the Wiener Werkstätte. He felt that no one man could ever fully administer all the Werkstätte's myriad fields of endeavor, let alone do all that and run the various Primavesi enterprises as well. His wife, on the other hand, considered the preservation of the Wiener Werkstätte not only an artistic, but a patriotic duty; to the end of her days, she never gave up hope of reviving it.

51. Grohmann was not, as reported by Schweiger (p. 122), a relative of Eugenie Primavesi, but of her husband; he had married a distant cousin. Mäda Primavesi (interview, January 3, 1986) suggests that it was her mother who encouraged Grohmann to try his hand at salvaging the Wiener Werkstätte but questions the extent to which he actually contributed either money or expertise to the enterprise.

52. Interview with Mäda Primvaesi, December 30, 1985.

53. "Alfred Kubin's Autobiography," in *The Other Side*, Denver Lind-ley, trans. (New York: Crown Publishers, 1967), p. lxi.

54. Burkhardt Rukschcio and Roland Schachel, *Adolf Loos* (Salzburg: Residenz Verlag, 1982), p. 199. In November 1914 Karl Kraus wrote a friend sadly that "Loos's conversation reveals a Teutonic fervor. Therefore communication is even more difficult than usual." Kraus's own famous essay, "In these Great Times," however, reveals no particularly clairvoyant knowledge of the actual outcome of the war, but only a grim dismay about its immediate cultural manifestations. Loos, Ludwig Wittgenstein, Kokoschka, and Schoenberg are among those who willingly accepted military service as their duty.

55. Schweiger, p. 106.

56. Egon Schiele, letter to Anton Peschka, March 2, 1917, in Christian M. Nebehay, *Egon Schiele, Leben, Briefe, Gedichte* (Salzburg: Residenz Verlag, 1979), p. 418.

57. Schweiger, p. 68.

III. ARCHITECTURE

1. Peter Vergo, *Art in Vienna 1898-1918* (London: Phaidon Press, Ltd., 1975), p. 118.

2. Otto Wagner, "Olbrich," in *Die Zeit*, August 9, 1908, pp. 4-5.

3. Eduard F. Sekler, *Josef Hoffmann, The Architectural Work* (Princeton: Princeton University Press, 1985), p. 18.

4. Ibid., p. 20.

5. Ibid., p. 41. Olbrich declared in 1898, "We must build a city, an entire city! Everything else means nothing! The government should give us a field, ... and there we want to show what we are capable of; in the entire settlement and to the last detail, everything dominated by the same spirit."

6. Werner Fenz, *Koloman Moser* (Salzburg: Residenz Verlag, 1984), p. 29.

7. *Deutsche Kunst und Dekoration*, Vol. XIX, October 1906-March 1907, p. 55.

8. Roger Billcliffe, *Mackintosh Furniture* (New York: E. P. Dutton, 1984), p. 9.

9. Fenz, pp. 33-34. The so-called Purkersdorf chair had been used in the Moser-designed Klimt installation in 1903 and was manufactured by Prag-Rudniker (a firm with which Moser worked) in several variations. These facts would tend to confirm a Moser attribution.

10. Mackintosh's *Haus eines Kunstfreundes* (never built) was designed in response to a competition sponsored by Alexander Koch's *Zeitschrift für Innendekoration* in 1901. Mackintosh received the purchase prize for his entry.

11. Carl E. Schorske (*Fin-de-Siècle Vienna, Politics and Culture* [New York: Alfred A. Knopf, 1980], p. 237) notes that the Secession's attempts to foster an international style were initially encouraged by the Habsburg regime because it was felt that native (i.e., "folk") styles would fuel the nationalistic divisiveness that threatened to tear the empire apart. The return to folk forms at the very moment when the empire was at the brink of destruction suggests a final attempt to forestall the inevitable by uniting behind the illusion that such forms constituted a national identity after all.

12. As used within the context of this book, the term "folkish" will be given a strictly stylistic interpretation, tacitly ignoring the political implications that Hitler would soon impart to the concept. However, one must not altogether forget that this concept of the "*Volk*," even as it applied to so seemingly innocuous an area as art, did in fact already invoke dangerous nationalistic tendencies.

13. Sekler, p. 129. Mäda Primavesi, the client's daughter, gives most of the credit for the idea of the house to Hoffmann, who she says thought it would be fun to employ regional vernacular motifs throughout the house.

14. Interview with Mäda Primavesi, December 20, 1985.

15. Alfred Kubin, *The Other Side*, Denver Lindley, trans. (New York: Crown Publishers, 1967), p. 13.

16. Burkhardt Rukschcio and Roland Schachel, *Adolf Loos* (Salzburg: Residenz Verlag, 1982), pp. 62-64.

17. Sekler, p. 29.

18. Adolf Loos, "Kulturentartung," (1908) in *Trotzdem* (Vienna: Georg Prachner Verlag, 1982), p. 77.

19. Karl Kraus, *Die Fackel*, No. 389-390, December 1913.

20. Schweiger, p. 10.

21. Ibid., p. 10.

22. *XIV. Ausstellung der Vereinigung Bildender Künstler Österreichs* (Vienna: Secession, 1902), pp. 9-10.

23. Armin Friedmann, "Sezessionistische Tafelfreuden, Das Tischleindeckdich der 'W.W.'", in *Neues Wiener Tageblatt*, October 16, 1906.

24. Vergo, p. 158.

25. Koloman Moser, "Bühnenbilder und Kostümentwürfe zu 'Der Musikant,'" in *Deutsche Kunst und Dekoration*, Vol. XXVII, 1910/11, p. 388.

26. In 1908 the Cabaret Fledermaus's first artistic director, Marc Henry, resigned, and there was a second change in management the following year. Each change brought a decline in quality, and in 1913 the space was taken over by the "Singspielhalle Feminina."

27. Sekler, p. 112.

28. Advertisement for J. & J. Kohn in *The Studio*, 1906, p. AD. II.

29. Like most Austrian industries, the bentwood firms were hard hit by World War I. Thonet's factories ended up outside the borders of the redefined nation. Kohn was absorbed by the firm Mundus, which in turn merged with Thonet in the mid-1920s.

30. Sekler, p. 484.

31. F. Servaes, "Kunst im Handwerk," in *Neue Freie Presse*, November 10, 1900.

32. Hermann Bahr, *Tagebücher 2* (Innsbruck/Vienna/Munich: Verlagsanstalt Tyrolia, 1919), pp. 262-263.

33. Ludwig Hevesi, *Altkunst-Neukunst, Wien 1894-1908* (Vienna: Verlagsbuchhandlung Carl Konegen, 1919), p. 227.

34. *Deutsche Kunst und Dekoration*, Vol. XXIV, April 1909-September 1909, pp. 85-88.

35. Schweiger, p. 207.

IV. FASHION

1. Attempts to definitely attribute particular garments to Hoffmann have been largely unsuccessful; however, he did publish an essay on "Das individuelle Kleid" (The Distinctive Dress) as early as 1908.

2. Austrian law does not permit the operation of a business such as a tailoring establishment without a formally licensed "master." Wimmer, trained as an architect, did not qualify, and it is perhaps for this reason that his name does not appear on the official fashion department documents. Marianne Zels, a "master" tailor, served as the titular head of the shop in the beginning; after the fashion division achieved "factory" status in 1914, the presence of such a master was no longer legally required.

3. Eduard Josef Wimmer-Wisgrill, letter to Josef Hoffmann, July 23, 1910, in Angela Völker, *Wiener Mode und Modefotografie* (Munich/Paris: Verlag Schneider-Henn, 1984), p. 16.

4. Werner J. Schweiger, *Wiener Werkstätte, Design in Vienna 1903-1932* (New York: Abbeville Press, 1984), p. 224.

5. Bertha Zuckerkandl, "Durch Kunst zur künstlerischen Mode," in *Wiener Allgemeine Zeitung*, March 15, 1913.

6. Völker, p. 47.

7. Schweiger, p. 42.

8. Schweiger, p. 220.

9. Völker, p. 8.

10. Schweiger, p. 187.

11. Ibid., p. 187.

12. According to James May, who has made an exhaustive study of the Wiener Werkstätte's American years, wallpaper installation was particularly problematical in the United States, where the level of craftsmanship was inferior to that in Austria.

13. Max Eisler, *Dagobert Peche* (Vienna/Leipzig, 1925).

14. Elisabeth Rücker, *Wiener Charme* (Nuremberg: Germanisches Nationalmuseum, 1984), p. 29.

15. Hermann Bahr, "Der englische Stil," in *Secession*, November 1900, p. 184.

16. Schweiger (p. 202) gives 1913 as the date of the merger between the Wiener Keramik and the Gmundner Keramik; Waltraud Neuwirth (*Österreichische Keramik des Jugendstils*, [Munich: Prestel Verlag, 1974], p. 209) gives the date as 1912.

17. Schweiger, p. 118.

18. Baudisch ran ceramics workshops in Germany and Austria; Wieselthier pursued her career in the United States; Flögl also had her own workshop and was active as a teacher, as were Jesser, Likarz and Rix.

19. This is confirmed by *The Studio* (1906, p. D-ix), and also by an early article on the coed group *Wiener Kunst im Hause* (*Das Interieur*, 1902, Vol. 3, pp. 97-98), that noted: "While the male members mainly look after and supervise the design of the rooms and the construction of the furniture, the women have taken over the production of the accessories."

20. Joseph Roth, *The Emperor's Tomb*, John Hoare, trans. (London: Chatto & Windus/The Hogarth Press, 1984), pp. 97-99.

21. Rücker, p. 5. Gretl Urban (interview, January 3, 1986) commented on the contrast between the living conditions of the Austrians after the war and the illusions their artists tried to create, noting that Peche occupied a house that was on the verge of collapse at the same time that he was producing his silver fantasies.

22. According to a statute recorded in 1895, the Kunstgewerbeschule consisted of four basic divisions: (1) the General Division, (2) master classes in architecture, painting and sculpture, (3) special crafts studios (for woodcarving, enamel, lacemaking, etc.), and (4) the Chemical Laboratory. Attendance was limited to a maximum of four (!) years in any one division, but within this rather lenient program, it appears that the students were more or less allowed to shape their own exact course of study. The length of time in the General Division seems to have varied from student to student, as did the length of time spent in a master class.

23. Rita Boley-Bolaffio, who studied under Hoffmann at the Kunstgewerbeschule during the war years (interview, November 5, 1985) claims that he showed up in the classroom no more than once a week. It is interesting to note that Hoffmann himself, in his first years at the Academy, had suffered under the tutelage of a teacher, Hasenauer, who was too busy to attend to his classes himself and instead delegated much of the day-to-day responsibility to an assistant.

24. Students had to pass a fairly rigorous exam (five days in duration, according to Rita Boley-Bolaffio) to get into the Kunstgewerbeschule, and Hoffmann's class of a half-dozen or so handpicked students was even more selective. During its heyday, the Kunstgewerbeschule also attracted foreign students, and competition was keen to get into the more desirable classes.

25. Koloman Moser, "Vom Schreibtisch und aus dem Atelier, Mein Werdegang," in *Koloman Moser* (Vienna: Hochschule für angewandte Kunst, 1979), p. 12.

IV. GRAPHIC ARTS

1. Werner J. Schweiger, "Koloman Moser, Eine biographische Skizze," in *Koloman Moser* (Vienna: Hochschule für angewandte Kunst, 1979), p. 21. Hereafter cited as Moser.

2. The system of identifying monograms can become exceedingly complex, as for instance when one must sort out the designer of the object, the craftsman/creator of the object, the designer of the decoration, and the craftsman/creator of the decoration.

3. For an exhaustive study of Wiener Werkstätte monograms and

their meaning, see Waltraud Neuwirth, *Wiener Werkstätte Schutzmarken I* (Vienna: Selbstverlag Dr. Waltraud Neuwirth, 1985).

4. Werner J. Schweiger, *Wiener Werkstätte, Design in Vienna 1903-1932* (New York: Abbeville Press, 1984), p. 43.

5. Eduard F. Sekler, *Josef Hoffmann, The Architectural Work* (Princeton: Princeton University Press, 1985), p. 167.

6. Daniele Baroni and Antonio D'Auria, *Josef Hoffmann und die Wiener Werkstätte* (Stuttgart: Deutsche Verlags-Anstalt, 1984), p. 46.

7. Many former Cizek students comment on the creative freedom that he encouraged, and yet the stylistic uniformity and almost self-conscious cuteness of much of the work somehow contradict this. What is certain is that Cizek brought out the "child" in children, and very few of his former students amounted to much as artists in later life. For further information on Cizek, see *Franz Cizek, Pionier der Kunsterziehung* (Vienna: Historisches Museum der Stadt Wien, 1985).

8. Schweiger (p. 177) gives 1907 as the year when the Wiener Werkstätte commenced its postcard series; Traude Hansen (*Die Postkarten der Wiener Werkstätte*, [Munich/Paris: Verlag Schneider-Henn, 1982], p. 11) gives the date of 1908. While it is true that the first numbered cards were published in connection with the 1908 Kunstschau, there were several unnumbered cards before this. Czeschka actually designed the first single Werkstätte card, a New Year's greeting, in 1905.

9. Schweiger, p. 178.

10. All biographical information on Richard Gerstl is based on Otto Kallir, "Richard Gerstl (1883-1908), Beiträge zur Dokumentation seines Lebens und Werkes," in *Mitteilungen der Österreichischen Galerie*, Vol. XVIII, No. 64 (1974).

11. Gerstl's painting *The Sisters*, one of the few to bear a confirmed date, was painted in 1905 and already shows strong Expressionist tendencies.

12. Werner Fenz, *Koloman Moser* (Salzburg: Residenz Verlag, 1984), p. 204.

13. Ibid., p. 205.

14. Gerstl's parents, unlike the families of Kokoschka and Schiele, were relatively well-to-do, and seem to willingly have paid for his art lessons and also a separate apartment/studio. Gerstl's early death leaves open the question of what might have happened had he lived to an age at which he might have been expected to support himself.

15. Werner J. Schweiger, *Der Junge Kokoschka* (Pöchlarn: Oskar Kokoschka Dokumentation Pöchlarn, 1983), p. 5. Hereafter cited as Pöchlarn.

16. Ludwig Goldscheider, *Kokoschka* (London: Phaidon Press, Ltd., 1963), p. 10.

17. Stephan Steinlein, "Ludwig Heinrich Jungnickel—München," in *Deutsche Kunst und Dekoration*, XVII, November 1905, p. 118.

18. Kokoschka himself always claimed that *Die träumenden Knaben* was done in 1906, or two years before its publication (thereby making it seem all the more revolutionary), and this assertion is repeated by Schweiger, p. 88. However, in Schweiger's earlier essay (Pöchlarn, pp. 31-32) he cites fairly conclusive evidence supporting a later date of 1907 or even 1908.

19. Unpublished letter, exhibited "Der junge Kokoschka," Oskar Kokoschka—Dokumentation Pöchlarn, June 24-September 25, 1983.

20. Pöchlarn, p. 7.

21. Fritz Wärndorfer, letter to C. O. Czeschka, February 4, 1908, in Pöchlarn, p. 42.

22. Jane Kallir, *Arnold Schoenberg's Vienna* (New York: Rizzoli International Publications, 1984), pp. 31-32.

23. As anticipated, *Die träumenden Knaben* was an economic disaster; the unsold copies were remaindered to the publisher Kurt Wolff, who reissued them in 1917 with a new title page.

24. Adolf Loos, "Bekenntnis zu Kokoschka," in *Oskar Kokoschka, Das gesammelte Werk* (Mannheim: Städtische Kunsthalle, 1931), pp. 2-3.

25. Goldscheider, p. 10.

26. Koloman Moser, undated letter to Gustav Klimt, in Fenz, p. 227. Of the four artists whom Moser mentions in his letter, three—Faistauer, Schiele and Wiegele—were members of the Neukunstgruppe—the group of artists who, together with Schiele, left the Academy in 1909 and exhibited together later that year. The third, Anton Kolig, actually received a travel stipend from Klimt and Moll in 1912, making it possible to date Moser's letter to around that time.

27. It is said that Klimt introduced Schiele to his favorite model, Valerie Neuzil; Klimt also introduced Schiele to one of his most important patrons, the industrialist August Lederer.